AN ACT

TO

REORGANIZE THE LOCAL GOVERNMENT

OF THE

CITY OF NEW YORK,

Passed April 30, 1873,

AS AMENDED;

With an Appendix containing the

SUPPLEMENTARY ACTS

Passed since the Year 1873.

NEW YORK:
MARTIN B. BROWN, PRINTER AND STATIONER,
Nos. 201, 203 & 205 William Street.

1876.

BOARD OF ALDERMEN.

AUGUST 10, 1876.

The following resolution was adopted:

Resolved, That one thousand copies of the act, chapter 335, Laws of 1873, commonly called the Charter, with the acts amendatory thereof, be printed in document form, for the use of the Mayor, members of the Common Council, and other city officials, under the direction of the Clerk.

FRANCIS J. TWOMEY,
Clerk.

CONTENTS OF CHARTER.

ARTICLE IX.

ARTICLE X.

ARTICLE XI.

ARTICLE XII.

ARTICLE XIII.

ARTICLE XIV.

ARTICLE XV.

ARTICLE XVI.

CONTENTS OF APPENDIX.

(H.)—CHAPTER 726, LAWS OF 1873.

(I.)—CHAPTER 839, LAWS OF 1873.

(J.)—CHAPTER 759, LAWS OF 1873.

(K.)—CHAPTER 631, LAWS OF 1875.

(L.)—CHAPTER 758, LAWS OF 1873.

(M.)—CHAPTER 308, LAWS OF 1874.

(N.)—CHAPTER 303, LAWS OF 1874.

(O.)—CHAPTER 326, LAWS OF 1873.

Chapter 335.

An Act to reorganize the local government of the city of New York.

Passed April 30, 1873; three-fifths being present.

The People of the State of New York, represented in Senate and Assembly, do enact as follows:

ARTICLE I.

The Corporate Powers.

Section 1. The corporation now existing and known by the name of "The Mayor, Aldermen, and Commonalty of the city of New York" shall continue to be a body politic and corporate, in fact and in name, by the same name, and have perpetual succession, with all the grants, powers, and privileges heretofore held by the mayor, aldermen, and commonalty of the city of New York, and not modified or repealed by the provisions of this act. **Corporate powers.**

ARTICLE II.

Of Legislative Powers.

Sec. 2. The legislative power of the said corporation shall continue to be vested in a board of aldermen and a board of assistant aldermen, who together shall form the **Legislative powers.**

Assistant aldermen, board of, abolished.

common council of the city of New York. The board of assistant aldermen is hereby abolished from and after the first day of January, eighteen hundred and seventy-five; and from and after that date the board of aldermen is hereby declared to be the common council, and shall solely possess the powers and perform all the duties by law conferred or imposed upon the board of aldermen, and board of assistant aldermen, the common council, or any one or more of them.

SEC. 3. Such aldermen shall be elected as hereinafter provided.

Aldermen, election of.

SEC. 4. [*As amended by sec.* 1, *chap.* 515, *laws of* 1874.] The board of aldermen now in office shall hold office until the first Monday in January, in the year eighteen hundred and seventy-five, the same being the term for which they were elected. There shall be twenty-two aldermen elected at the general state election which shall occur in the year eighteen hundred and seventy-four, three of whom shall be elected in each senate district, except the eighth senate district, and shall be residents of the district in which they are elected, but no voter shall vote for more than two of said aldermen. In the territory comprised within the eighth senate district, and the twenty-third and twenty-fourth wards, there shall be elected four aldermen, and the aldermen to be elected in said district may reside either in said eighth senate district or in the twenty-third and

Aldermen in twenty-third and twenty-fourth wards.

twenty-fourth wards, but no voter shall vote for more than three of the said aldermen. There shall also be elected six aldermen at large to be voted for on a separate ballot, but no voter shall vote for more than four of the said aldermen at large, and the voters of the twenty-third and twenty-fourth wards of said city are hereby authorized and empowered to vote for aldermen at large. The members of the board of aldermen shall hold office for the space of one year, and shall take office on the first Monday in January, next succeeding their election, at noon. Annually thereafter, at the general state election, there shall be elected a full board of aldermen as hereinbefore provided. Any vacancy now existing or which may hereafter occur in *either* the board of aldermen* by reason of the death or resignation, or of any other cause, of a member of either of said boards, shall be filled by election by the board in which such vacancy exists or shall arise, by a vote of a majority of all the members elected to said board; and the person so elected to fill any such vacancy shall serve until the first day of January, at noon, next succeeding the first general election occurring not less than thirty days after the happening of such vacancy, but not beyond the expiration of the term in which the vacancy shall occur; and at such election a person shall be elected to serve the remainder, if any, of such unexpired term. From and after the termination of the term of

Aldermen at large.

Annual election.

Vacancies, how filled.

* So in the original.

office of the board of assistant aldermen, as herein provided, the board of aldermen alone shall constitute the common council and shall exercise the entire legislative powers of the said city.*

Quorum.

SEC. 5. The boards shall meet in separate chambers, and a majority of each shall constitute a quorum; but the comptroller, the commissioner of public works, the corporation counsel, and the president of each department shall be entitled to seats in each board, and to notice of its meetings, and shall have the right to participate in the discussions of each board, but in nowise shall be considered as members of either board, and shall not have the right to vote in either board.

SEC. 6. Each board shall—

Officers, how elected.

1. Choose a president from its own members by a call of the names of the members of the board, upon which call each member shall announce his choice, and when once chosen he can be removed before the expiration of his term as alderman or assistant alderman only, by a vote, taken by a call of ayes or noes, of four-fifths of all the members of the board of which he shall have been chosen president;

Powers and duties.

2. Appoint a clerk and other officers;

3. Determine the rules of its own proceedings;

4. Be the judge of the election returns and qualifications

*See Appendix, A, B, and C.

of its own members, subject, however, to the review of any court of competent jurisdiction;

5. Keep a journal of its proceedings;

6. Sit with open doors;

7. Have the authority to compel the attendance of absent members, and to punish its members for disorderly behavior, and to expel any member, with the concurrence of two-thirds of the members elected to the board.

But no alderman or assistant alderman shall sit or act as a magistrate in any judicial matter or proceeding. This section, however, shall not be construed to require or authorize a reorganization of the existing board of aldermen, or board of assistant aldermen. **Aldermen denied judicial powers.**

SEC. 7. [*As amended by sec. 2, chap. 757, laws of* 1873.] Every member expelled from either board shall thereby forfeit all his rights and powers as alderman or assistant alderman.*

SEC. 8. [*As amended by sec. 3, chap. 757, laws of* 1873.] The stated and occasional meetings of each board shall be regulated by its own resolutions and rules, and both boards may meet at the same time or on different days, as they may severally deem expedient. **Meetings.**

SEC. 9. Every legislative act of the common council shall be by resolution or ordinance; and every ordinance **All acts to be approved by Mayor.**

*See Appendix, D.

or resolution shall, before it shall take effect, be presented, duly certified, to the mayor for his approval.

SEC. 10. [*As amended by sec. 4, chap. 757, laws of* 1873.] The mayor shall return such ordinance or resolution to the board in which it originated within ten days after receiving it, or at the next meeting of such board after the expiration of said ten days.

Veto.

SEC. 11. If he approve it, he shall sign it. If he disapprove it, he shall specify his objections thereto in writing. If he do not return it with such disapproval within the time above specified, it shall take effect as if he had approved it.

Veto to be entered in journal.

SEC. 12. Such objections of the mayor shall be entered at large on the journal of the board in which said ordinance or resolution originated.

Proceedings in case of a veto.

SEC. 13. The board to which such ordinance or resolution shall have been returned, with objections, shall, after ten days and within fifteen days after such ordinance or resolution shall have been so returned, proceed to reconsider and vote upon the same; and if the same shall, on reconsideration, be again passed by both boards by the votes of at least two-thirds of all the members elected to each board, but in no case by a less vote than was necessary on its first passage, it shall take effect. But if the ordinance or resolution shall fail to receive, upon the first vote thereon, such number of affirmative votes, it shall be deemed finally lost. In all cases the vote shall be taken

Votes, how taken.

by ayes and noes, and the names of the persons voting for or against its passage, on such reconsideration, shall be entered in the journal of each board. In case an ordinance or resolution shall embrace more than one distinct subject, the mayor may approve the provisions relating to one or more subjects and disapprove the others. In such case, those which he shall approve shall become effective, and those which he shall not approve shall be reconsidered by the board, and shall only become effective if again passed as above provided.

Ordinances may originate in either board.

SEC. 14. Any ordinance or resolution may originate in either board, and when it shall have passed one board, may be rejected or amended in the other; but no ordinance or resolution shall be passed except by a vote of the majority of all the members elected to the board, and no ordinance or resolution shall be valid unless it shall receive the assent of both boards within the term fixed by law to such boards. In case any ordinance or resolution involves the expenditure of money or the laying of an assessment, the lease of real estate or franchises, the votes of three-fourths of all the members elected to each board shall become necessary to its passage. No money shall be expended for any celebration, procession, funeral ceremony, reception or entertainment of any kind, or on any occasion, unless by the votes of four-fifths of all the members elected to each board. No additional allowance beyond the legal claim which shall exist under any contract with the corporation, or with any department or officer thereof, or for any

Expenditure limited.

services on its account or in its employment, shall ever be passed by the common council, except by the unanimous vote thereof; but, in all cases, the provisions of any such contract shall determine the amount of any claim thereunder or in connection therewith, against the said corporation, or the value of any such services.

Clerk of board, his powers and duties.

SEC. 15. [*As amended by sec.* 5, *chap.* 757, *laws of* 1873.] The clerk of the board of aldermen shall, by virtue of his office, be clerk of the common council and of the board of supervisors, and shall perform all the duties heretofore performed by the clerk of the common council, except such as shall be assigned to the clerk of the board of assistant aldermen, without additional compensation to that paid him as clerk of the board of aldermen. It shall be his duty to keep open for inspection, at all reasonable times, the records and minutes of the proceedings of said boards. He shall keep the seal of the city, and his signature shall be necessary to all leases, grants and other documents, as under existing laws. The clerk of each board shall, subject to the rules of the board, appoint and remove at pleasure deputy clerks in his department and fix their salaries.

Deputy clerks.

The deputy clerks and other officers of the board of aldermen shall be officers of the board of supervisors, which shall have no separate officers or subordinates, and such clerks and officers shall receive no additional compensation for duties performed for the supervisors. The aggregate amount of salaries paid to the clerks and officers of the board of aldermen, including the salary of the clerk, shall not exceed twenty-five thousand dollars in any one year, and the aggregate amount of salaries paid to the clerks and officers of the board of assistant aldermen, including the salary of the clerk, shall not exceed fifteen thousand dollars in any one year. Salaries.

SEC. 16. Immediately after the adjournment of each meeting of either board, it shall be the duty of the clerk of such board to prepare a brief abstract, omitting all technical and formal details, of all resolutions and ordinances introduced or passed, and of all recommendations of committees, and of all final proceedings, as well as full copies of all messages from the mayor, and all reports of departments or officers. He shall at once transmit the same to the person appointed to supervise the publication of the City Record. No resolution or ordinance providing for or contemplating the alienation or appropriation or leasing any property of the city, terminating the lease of any property or franchise, or the making of any specific improvement, or the appropriation or expenditure of public moneys, or authorizing the incurring of any expense or the taxing or assessing of property in the city, shall be passed or adopted by either board until at least five days after such abstract of its provisions shall have been published. No such ordinance or resolution shall be approved by the mayor until three days after such abstract shall have been so published after its passage; but if an

To prepare and publish abstract of meetings.

Resolutions to be published.

abstract of any resolution or ordinance shall have been once published after its introduction, it shall not thereafter be necessary to publish the same again, but only to refer to the date and page of the former in the City Record, and to state the amendments, if any, made thereto. In all cases the yeas and nays upon the final passage of the resolution or ordinance shall be published. The comptroller shall cause a continuous series of the City Record to be bound as completed quarterly, and to be deposited, with his certificate thereon, in the office of the register of deeds in the city and county of New York, in the county clerk's office and in the office of the clerk of the common council, and copies of the contents of any part of the same, certified by such register, county clerk, or clerk of the common council, shall be received in judicial proceedings as prima facie evidence of the truth of the contents thereof.

City Record to be certified and deposited.

County clerk's office.

Powers of common council.

SEC. 17. The common council shall have power to make, continue, modify, and repeal such ordinances, regulations and resolutions as may be necessary to carry into effect any and all of the powers now vested in or by this act conferred upon the corporation, and shall have the power to enforce obedience to such ordinances and observance thereof, by ordaining penalties for each and every violation thereof, in such sums as it may deem expedient, not exceeding one hundred dollars; and shall have power to make such ordinances, not inconsistent with law and the constitution of this state, and with such penalties, in the matter, and for the purposes following, in addition to other powers elsewhere specially granted, namely:

1. To regulate traffic and sales in the streets, highways, roads and public places. Powers specified.

2. To regulate the use of the streets, highways, roads and public places by foot passengers, animals, vehicles, cars and locomotives. Use of streets.

2.* To regulate the use of sidewalks, and prevent the extension of building fronts and house fronts within the stoop lines. Use of sidewalks.

4. To prevent encroachments upon and obstructions to the streets, highways, roads and public places, not including parks, and to authorize and require the commissioners of public works to remove the same, but they shall have no power to authorize the placing or continuing of any encroachment or obstruction upon any street or sidewalk, except the temporary occupation thereof, during the erection or repair of a building on a lot opposite the same. Obstructions.

5. To regulate the opening of street surfaces, the laying of gas and water mains, the building and repairing of sewers, and the erecting of gas-lights. Opening streets.

6. To regulate the numbering of the houses and lots in the streets and avenues, and the naming of the streets, To number houses.

*So in original.

avenues and public places; but it shall not be lawful for the said board to number or renumber any houses, in any street, avenue, alley, lane, road, way or public place, or to in anywise change or alter any such numbering or the name of any street, avenue or public place, save between the first day of December of any year and the first day of May next ensuing.

Garbage, etc.

7. To regulate and prevent the throwing or depositing of ashes, offal, dirt or garbage in the streets.

Cleaning streets.

8. To regulate the cleaning of the streets, avenues, sidewalks and gutters, and removing ice and snow from them.

Use of streets.

9. To regulate the use of the streets and sidewalks for signs, sign-posts, awnings, awning-posts, horse-troughs, urinals, telegraph-posts and other purposes.

10. [*As amended by sec.* 6, *chap.* 757, *Laws of* 1873.] To provide for and regulate street pavements, crosswalks, curbstones, gutterstones, sidewalks, and the grade of streets, and to provide for regulating, grading, flagging, curbing, guttering and lighting streets, roads, places and avenues.

To regulate street traffic, etc.

11. To regulate public cries, advertising noises, steam whistles, and ringing bells in the streets, and to control and limit traffic in the streets, avenues and public places.

12. In relation to street beggars, vagrants and mendicants.

13. In relation to the use of guns, pistols, firearms, firecrackers, fireworks, and detonating works of all descriptions within the city.

14. In relation to intoxication, fighting and quarreling in the streets.

15. In relation to places of public amusement.

16. In relation to exhibiting banners, placards or flags in or across the streets or from houses or other buildings.

17. In relation to the exhibition of advertisements or handbills along the streets, avenues and public places.

18. In relation to the construction, repairs and use of vaults, cisterns, areas, hydrants pumps and sewers.

19. In relation to partition fences and walls.

20. In relation to the construction, repair, care and use of markets.

Licensing hackmen.

21. In relation to the licensing and business of public cartmen, truckmen, hackmen, cabmen, expressmen, car-drivers, boatmen, pawnbrokers, junk dealers, hawkers, peddlers and venders, and all licenses shall be according to an established form and regularly numbered, and be duly registered in the office of the mayor.

22. In relation to the inspection and sealing of weights and measures, and enforcing the keeping and use of proper weights and measures by venders.

23. In relation to the inspection, weighing and measur-

ing of fire-wood, coal, hay and straw, and the cartage of the same.

24. In relation to the mode and manner of suing for, collecting and keeping accounts of the city and county, and disposing of the penalties provided for a violation of all ordinances.

Public fountains.

25. In relation to the erection and repair of public fountains for the use of man and animals, at convenient points along the streets and avenues and public places.

26. By resolution to require the commissioner of public works to do any work or take any action proper for carrying into effect the powers of the common council. The ordinances of the common council shall, as far as practicable, be reduced to a code, and be published as such in the City Record.

To impose taxes.

SEC. 18. The common council shall have no power to impose taxes or assessments, or borrow money, or contract debts, or loan the credit of the city, or take or make a lease of any real estate or franchise, save at a reasonable rent and for a period not exceeding five years, unless specially authorized so to do by act of the legislature.

ARTICLE III.

Of the Executive Power.

SEC. 19. The executive power of the corporation shall be vested in the mayor and the officers of the departments herein created.

SEC. 20. [*As amended by sec. 7, chap. 757, laws of 1873.*] The mayor in office on April twenty-ninth, eighteen hundred and seventy-three, shall hold office until the first day of January, in the year eighteen hundred and seventy-five. The mayor shall be the chief executive officer of the corporation; shall be elected at a general election, and hold his office for the term of two years, commencing on the first day of January next after his election. The first election for mayor under this act shall be at the general election in November, in the year eighteen hundred and seventy-four.

Executive power.

Mayor.

SEC. 21. Whenever the mayor shall be under suspension, or there shall be a vacancy in the office of mayor, or whenever, by reason of sickness or absence from the city, he shall be prevented from attending to the duties of his office, the president of the board of aldermen shall act as mayor, and possess all the rights and powers of mayor during such suspension, disability or absence. In case of a vacancy he shall so act until the first Monday of January succeeding the next general election, and at the general election next to be held, at which a mayor can be chosen, but not within ten days after the occurrence of any such vacancy, a mayor shall be chosen for the unexpired term for which such officer was chosen, and no special election shall be held to fill such vacancy. It shall not be lawful for the president of the board of aldermen when acting as mayor, in consequence of the

President of board may act as mayor.

Acting mayor not to exercise certain powers.

sickness or absence from the city of the person elected, to exercise any power of appointment to or removal from office, unless such sickness or absence of the mayor shall have continued ten days, nor to sign, approve, or disapprove any ordinance or resolution, unless such sickness or absence shall have continued the same period.

Temporary chairman in case of vacancy.

SEC. 22. In case of a vacancy in the office of mayor, the aldermen may elect a temporary chairman to preside over their meetings, who shall possess, during such vacancy, the powers and perform the duties of the president of the board.

SEC. 23. It shall be the duty of the mayor:

Mayor to make annual statement.

1. To communicate to the common council, at least once a year, a general statement of the finances, government and improvements of the city.

2. To recommend to the common council all such measures as he shall deem expedient.

3. To keep himself informed of the doings of the several departments.

4. To be vigilant and active in causing the ordinances of the city and laws of the state to be executed and enforced, and for that purpose he may call together for consultation and co-operation all heads of departments.

5. And generally to perform all such duties as may be prescribed for him by the city ordinances and the laws of the state.

SEC. 24. The mayor may appoint such clerks and subordinates as he may require to aid him in the discharge of his official duties, and shall render to the board of aldermen, every three months, an account of the expenses and receipts of his office, and therein shall state, in detail, the amounts paid and agreed to be paid by him for salaries to such clerks and subordinates respectively, and the general nature of their duties, which shall be published in the City Record. The aggregate expenses incurred by him for such purposes shall not exceed, in any one year, the sum of twenty thousand dollars. **Mayor to appoint his clerks.**

SEC. 25. The mayor shall nominate, and, by and with the consent of the board of aldermen, appoint the heads of departments and all commissioners (save commissioners of public instruction, and also save and except the following named commissioners and officers who held office as such on the first day of January, in the year one thousand eight hundred and seventy-three, that is to say, the comptroller, the commissioner of public works, the counsel to the corporation, the president of the department of public parks, and the president of the department of police, which said comptroller, commissioners and counsel to the corporation shall hold their respective offices, as such comptroller, commissioners and counsel to the corporation aforesaid, until the expiration of their respective terms of office for which they were appointed, unless removed for cause as herein provided), and the said mayor shall in like manner appoint all members of any board or com- **Mayor shall nominate heads of departments.**

mission authorized to superintend the erection or repair of any building belonging to or to be paid for by the city, whether named in any law or appointed by any local authority, and also members of any other local board and all other officers not elected by the people,* including the commissioner of jurors, whose appointment is not in this act excepted or otherwise provided for. Every head of department and person in this section named, except as herein otherwise provided, shall hold his office for the term of six years, and in each case until a person is duly appointed in his place. The terms of office of all such heads of departments and persons other than those first appointed shall commence on the first day of May, but the heads of departments, consisting of boards of commissioners first appointed after the passage of this act, shall, except as herein otherwise expressly provided, be appointed, for two, four and six years respectively, and except that the commissioners of police first appointed as aforesaid shall hold their offices for one, two, three and five years respectively. The persons first appointed shall take office on the expiration of the terms of office of the present incumbents, as hereinafter provided, and shall hold their offices until the first day of May in the year in which it is herein provided that their respective terms shall expire. All nominations to any office or offices which, by this act, the mayor is authorized or empowered to nominate a person or persons to in place of any present incumbent or incumbents, shall be made to the board of

Terms of office.

Nominations.

* See Appendix, D.

aldermen within twenty days after the passage of this act, and any such nomination or nominations to fill any vacancy which shall hereafter occur by reason of the expiration of the term of office of any officer, or from any other cause, and which shall not be created by anything in this act, providing for the termination of the term of office of any officer or person now in office, shall be made to the board of aldermen, within ten days from the day of the date of any such vacancy, and any person who shall be appointed to fill any such vacancy shall hold his office for the unexpired term of his predecessor. The mayor may be removed from office by the governor in the same manner as sheriffs, except that the governor may direct the inquiry provided by law to be conducted by the attorney-general; and after charges have been received by the governor he may, pending the investigation, suspend the mayor for a period not exceeding thirty days. The heads of all departments, including those retained as above, and all other persons whose appointment is in this section provided for, may be removed by the mayor for cause, and after opportunity to be heard, subject, however, before such removal shall take effect, to the approval of the governor, expressed in writing. The mayor shall, in all cases, communicate to the governor, in writing, his reasons for such removal. Whenever a removal is so effected, the mayor shall, upon the demand of the officer removed, make, in writing, a public statement of the reasons therefor. No officer so removed shall

Mayor, how removed.

Heads of departments, how removed.

be again appointed to the same office during the same term of office.

[*As amended by sec.* 3, *chap.* 300, *laws of* 1874.]

Mayor to fill vacancy.

The mayor of said city shall hereafter appoint, without confirmation of the board of aldermen, a person or persons to fill any vacancy or vacancies which now exists or may hereafter occur from death, resignation or cause other than the expiration of the full term in any office to which, of the provisions of the twenty-fifth section of chapter three hundred and thirty-five of the laws of eighteen hundred and seventy-three, he is empowered to appoint by and with the consent of the board of aldermen.*

City departments.

SEC. 26. There shall be the following other departments in said city:

Finance department.
Law department.
Police department.
Department of public works.
Department of public charities and correction.
Fire department.
Health department.
Department of public works. †
Department of docks.

* See Appendix, F. † So in original.

Department of taxes and assessments.

Department of buildings.

SEC. 27. The said departments shall, once in three months, and at such other times as the mayor may direct, make to him, in such form and under such rules as he may prescribe, reports of the operations and action of the same and each of them, which reports shall be published in the City Record. The said departments shall always, when required by the mayor, furnish to him such information as he may demand, within such reasonable time as he may direct.

To report quarterly to mayor.

SEC. 28. The heads of all departments (except as otherwise herein specifically provided) shall have power to appoint and remove all chiefs of bureaus (except the chamberlain), as also all clerks, officers, employees, and subordinates in their respective departments, except as herein otherwise specially provided, without reference to the tenure of office of any existing appointee. But no regular clerk or head of a bureau shall be removed until he has been informed of the cause of the proposed removal, and has been allowed an opportunity of making an explanation; and in every case of a removal, the true grounds thereof shall be forthwith entered upon the records of the department or board. In case of removal, a statement, showing the reason therefor, shall be filed in the department. The number and duties of all officers and clerks, employees and subordinates in every department, except as otherwise herein specifically provided,

Heads of departments to appoint the clerks, etc.

Clerks, how removed.

Duties of clerks.

with their respective salaries, whether now fixed by special law or otherwise, shall be such as the heads of the respective departments shall designate and approve; but subject, also, to the revision of the board of apportionment; provided, however, that the aggregate expense thereof shall not exceed the total amount duly appropriated to the respective departments for such purposes. Any head of department may, with the consent of the board of apportionment, consolidate any two or more bureaus established by law, and may change the duties of any bureau; and it shall be the duty of the head of the finance department to bring together all officers and bureaus authorized to receive money for taxes, assessments or arrears, in such manner that the payment of the same can be made, as nearly as practicable, at one time and place, and in one office.

ARTICLE V.

Of the Finance Department.

Finance. SEC. 29. The finance department shall have control of the fiscal concerns of the corporation. It shall prescribe the forms of keeping and rendering all city accounts, and, except as herein otherwise provided, the manner in which all salaries shall be drawn, and the mode by which all creditors, officers and employees of the corporation shall be paid. All payments by or on behalf of the corporation shall be made through the proper disbursing officer of the department of finance, on vouchers to be filed in said department, by means of warrants drawn on the chamberlain by the comptroller, and countersigned by the mayor. The comptroller may require any person presenting for settlement an account or claim against the corporation to be sworn before him touching such account or claim, and when so sworn to answer orally as to any facts relative to the justness of such account or claim. The power hereby given the comptroller to settle and adjust such claims shall not be construed to give such settlement and adjustment the binding effect of a judgment or decree, nor to authorize the comptroller to dispute the amount of any salary established by or under the authority of any officer or department authorized to establish the same nor to question the due performance of his duties by such officer, except when necessary to prevent fraud. The comptroller shall not reduce the rate of interest upon any taxes or assessments below the amount fixed by law. No contract hereafter made, the expense of the execution of which is not by law or ordinance in whole or in part to be paid by assessments upon the property benefited, shall be binding or of any force or effect unless the comptroller shall indorse thereon his certificate that there remains unexpended and unapplied, as herein provided, a balance of the appropriation applicable thereto sufficient to pay the estimated expense of executing such contract as certified by the officer making the same.

Claimants to be sworn.

Contracts, how binding.

[*Amended by sec.* 8, *chap.* 757, *laws of* 1873.]

But this provision shall not apply to work done, or supplies furnished, not involving the expenditure of more than one thousand dollars, pursuant to section ninety-one of this act. It shall be the duty of the comptroller to make such indorsement upon every such contract so presented to him, if there remains unapplied and unexpended such amount so specified by the officer making the contract, and to thereafter hold and retain such sum to pay the expense incurred until the said contract shall be fully performed. And such indorsement shall be sufficient evidence of such appropriation in any action. The comptroller shall furnish to each head of department, weekly, a statement of the unexpended balance of the appropriation for his department; wages and salaries, including payments for the board of education, may be made upon pay-rolls, upon which each person named thereon shall separately receipt for the amount paid to such person, and in every case of payment upon a pay-roll, the warrant for the aggregate amount of wages and salaries included therein, may be made payable to the superintendent, principal teacher, foreman or other officer designated for the purpose.

Comptroller to furnish weekly statement.

Pay-rolls.

Comptroller, term of office.

SEC. 30. The head of the finance department shall be called the comptroller of the city of New York, and shall hold his office for four years, and until his successor shall be appointed, unless sooner removed as herein provided.

Accounts subject to revision.

SEC. 31. All accounts rendered to or kept in the other departments shall be subject to the inspection and revision of the officers of this department; and, subject to the conditions aforesaid, it shall settle and adjust all claims in favor of or against the corporation, and all accounts in which the corporation is concerned as debtor or creditor, but, in adjusting and settling such claims, it shall, as far as practicable, be governed by the rules of law and principles of equity which prevail in courts of justice.

Deputy comptroller.

SEC. 32. The comptroller of the city of New York shall appoint, and at pleasure remove, for cause to be stated in writing and published in said City Record, a deputy comptroller. The said deputy comptroller shall, in addition to his other powers, possess every power and perform all and every duty belonging to the office of comptroller, as herein provided, whenever the said comptroller shall, for reasons to be stated to the mayor in writing, by due written authority, and during a period of time not extending beyond three months, nor beyond his term of office, and to be specified in such authority, designate and authorize the said deputy comptroller to possess the power and perform the duty aforesaid, and such designation and authority shall be duly filed in and remain of record in the finance department and in the mayor's office. The said deputy comptroller shall possess the like authority in case of the disability of the comptroller upon the like designation of the mayor, which shall be filed and remain of record as aforesaid;

Powers and duties.

but such authority may at any time be terminated in the same manner as it was created.

Bureaus.

SEC. 33. There shall be eight bureaus in this department:

Collection of revenues.

1. A bureau for the collection of the revenue accruing from rents, and interest on bonds and mortgages, revenue arising from the use or sale of property belonging to or managed by the city; the chief officer of which bureau shall be called the "collector of the city revenue."

2. A bureau for the collection of taxes; the chief officer of which shall be called the "receiver of taxes," and he shall have all the powers, and perform all the duties heretofore prescribed by law for the receiver of taxes.

3. A bureau for the collection of arrears of taxes and assessments and of water rents; the chief officer of which shall be called "clerk of arrears."

4. An auditing bureau, which, under the supervision of the comptroller, shall audit, revise, and settle all accounts in which the city is concerned as debtor or creditor, and which shall keep an account of each claim for or against the corporation, and of the sums allowed upon each, and certify the same to the comptroller, with the reasons for the allowance; the chief officer of which shall be called "auditor of accounts."

5. A bureau of licenses; the chief officer of which shall be called "register of licenses."

6. A bureau of markets; the chief officer of which shall be called "superintendent of markets."

7. A bureau for the reception of all moneys paid into the treasury of the city, and for the payment of money on warrants drawn by the comptroller and countersigned by the mayor; the chief officer of which shall be called the "chamberlain."

8. A bureau for the collection of assessments; the chief officer of which shall be called "collector of assessments," and his assistants "deputy collectors of assessments."

SEC. 34. The chamberlain shall be appointed in the same manner as heads of departments, and shall hold his office for four years, unless sooner removed, as herein provided. He shall, within ten days after receiving notice of his appointment and confirmation, and before he enters upon his office, give a bond to the city in the sum of one million dollars, with not less than four sufficient sureties, to be approved by the comptroller, conditioned that he will faithfully execute the duties of his office. Such bond shall be deemed to extend to the faithful execution of the duties of the office until a new appointment shall be made and confirmed, and the person so appointed enters upon the performance of his duties. Said chamberlain shall exhibit to the common council at its first meeting in the

Appointment of chamberlain.

To give bond.

Duties of.

month succeeding that in which he enters upon the execution of his office, an exact statement of the balance in the treasury to the credit of the city, with a summary of the receipts and payments of the treasury during the preceding year, and since the last preceding report required by law, if more than a year shall have elapsed since such report. He shall receive all moneys which shall, from time to time, be paid into the treasury of the city. He shall deposit all moneys which shall come into his hands on account of the city on the day of the receipt thereof, or on the business day next succeeding, in such banks and trust companies as shall have been designated as deposit banks by the chamberlain and mayor jointly; but not exceeding two millions dollars shall be on deposit at any time in any one bank or trust company. The money so deposited shall be placed to the account of the chamberlain, and he shall keep a bank book, in which shall be entered his accounts of deposits in, and moneys drawn from, the banks and trust companies in which the deposits shall be made. The said banks and trust companies shall, respectively, transmit to the comptroller a weekly statement of the moneys which shall be received and paid by them on account of the city treasury. The chamberlain shall pay all warrants drawn on the treasury by the comptroller and countersigned by the mayor, and no moneys shall be paid out of the treasury except on the warrant of the comptroller so countersigned. No such warrant shall be signed by the comptroller or countersigned by the mayor, except upon vouchers for the

Weekly statement of deposits.

expenditure of the amount named therein, examined and allowed by the auditor, approved by the comptroller, and filed in the department of finance, except in the case of judgments, in which case a transcript thereof shall be filed, nor except such warrant shall be authorized by law or ordinance, and shall refer to the law or ordinance and to the appropriation under and from which it is drawn. The chamberlain shall not draw any moneys from said banks or trust companies, unless by checks subscribed by him as chamberlain and countersigned by the comptroller; and no moneys shall be paid by either of the said banks or trust companies on account of the treasury except upon such checks. The chamberlain shall exhibit his bank book to the comptroller on the first Tuesday of every month, and oftener when required. The accounts of the city treasury shall be annually closed on the last day of November, and shall be examined in the month of December in said year by the commissioners of accounts. Such commissioners shall examine the accounts and vouchers of all moneys received into and paid out of the city treasury during the year ending on the last day of November next preceding such examination, and shall certify and report to the mayor and the common council, in the following month of January, the amount of moneys received into the treasury during such year, the amount of moneys paid out during the same period by virtue of warrants drawn on the treasury by the comptroller, the amount of moneys received by the chamberlain who shall be in office at the time of such examination if he entered

Monthly statement.

Annual account.

upon the execution of his duties since the last preceding report, the balance in the treasury on the last day of November preceding such examination, the amount of moneys borrowed for or on the credit of the city during such year, and the amount of bonds of the city issued during such year, with the purposes for which and the authority under which such bonds were issued. Such commissioners shall also compare the warrants drawn by the comptroller on the treasury during the year ending on the last day of November preceding such examination, with the several laws and ordinances under which the same shall purport to have been drawn, and shall in like manner certify and report whether the comptroller had power to draw such warrants; and if any shall be found which in their opinion he had no power to draw, they shall specify the same in their report, with their reasons for such opinion.

Warrants to be compared.

SEC. 35. [*As amended by sec.* 1, *chap.* 129, *laws of* 1875.] The said chamberlain and mayor and the comptroller of the city of New York shall, by a majority vote, by written notice to the comptroller, designate the banks or trust companies in which all moneys of the mayor, aldermen, and commonalty of the said city and county of New York shall be deposited, and may, by like notice, in writing, from time to time, change the banks or trust companies thus designated; but no such bank or trust company shall be designated unless its officers shall agree to pay

Banks, how chosen.

into the city treasury interest on the daily balances at a rate to be fixed by the mayor and chamberlain and the said comptroller of the city of New York by a majority vote, which rate shall not be less than two and one-half per cent. The said chamberlain shall keep books showing the receipts of moneys from all sources, and designating the sources of the same, and also showing the amounts paid from time to time on acccount of the several appropriations; and no warrant shall be paid on account of any appropriation after the amount authorized to be raised for that specific purpose shall have been expended. The said chamberlain shall once in each week report in writing to the mayor and to the comptroller all moneys received by him, the amounts of all warrants paid by him since his last report, and the amount remaining to the credit of the city and county of New York respectively. The said chamberlain shall receive the sum of thirty thousand dollars annually and no more for all his services as chamberlain of said city and as county treasurer of the county of New York in lieu of salary and of all interest, fees, commissions and emoluments; and all such interest, fees, commissions and emoluments shall be accounted for and paid over by him to the city treasury. He may appoint and remove at pleasure a deputy chamberlain and such clerks and assistants as may be necessary, whose salaries, together with all the expenses of his office, shall be paid wholly by him, and shall in no case be

Weekly report.

Salary.

Clerks.

Commissions. a public charge. The commissions provided by law and received by him for receiving and paying over the state taxes and all interest accrued on deposits shall be paid by him to the commissioners of the sinking fund.*

ARTICLE VI.

Of the Law Department.

SEC. 36. The law department shall have the charge and conduct of all the law business of the corporation and its departments, and of all law business in which the city of New York shall be interested, except as herein otherwise provided; the charge and conduct of the legal proceedings necessary in widening, opening or altering streets, and the preparation of all leases, deeds and other legal paper connected with any department. No officer or department, except as herein otherwise provided, shall have or employ any attorney or counsel, but it shall be the duty of the law department to furnish to every department and officer such advice and legal assistance as counsel or attorney, in or out of court, as may be required by such officer or department; and for that purpose he may assign an attorney to any department that he shall deem to need the same, and may appoint the attorney for the collection of personal taxes.

Counsel to corporation.

Attorneys, when appointed.

SEC. 37. The head of the law department shall be

* See Appendix, E.

called "counsel to the corporation." He shall hold his office for four years, and until his successor is appointed, unless sooner removed, as herein provided.

SEC. 38. There shall be two bureaus in this department, the chief officer of one of which shall be called the "corporation attorney," and the chief officer of the other of which shall be called the "public administrator." Such chief officers shall not receive to their own use any fees or emoluments in addition to their salaries, and they shall pay into the treasury all costs and commissions received by them from any source whatever; such payments shall be made monthly, and shall be accompanied by a sworn statement, in such form as the comptroller shall prescribe, and that such statement, with a detailed list of costs, commissions, fines and penalties collected, shall be published in the City Record monthly, as furnished. All actions to recover penalties for a violation of any law or ordinance shall be brought in the name of the mayor, aldermen and the commonalty of the city of New York, and not in that of any department, and shall be conducted by the corporation attorney, subject to the control of the corporation counsel. All fees received in said action shall be paid into the treasury of the city. The counsel to the corporation shall, once in three months, report to the comptroller the names of parties to, and the objects of, all suits pending in his department, when commenced, and the number decided or ended, and in what manner, during the past three months.

Bureaus.

Actions, how brought.

Fees.

Quarterly report.

ARTICLE VII.

Of the Police Department.*

Police commissioners.

SEC. 39. [*As amended by sec.* 1, *chap.* 300, *laws of* 1874.] The police department shall have for its head a board to consist of four persons, to be known as police commissioners of the city of New York, who shall, except those first appointed, hold their offices for six years, unless sooner removed as herein provided. The office of the police commissioner of the city of New York, whose term of office expires on the first day of May, eighteen hundred and seventy-four, is hereby abolished on and after said date; the police department, on and after the first day of May, eighteen hundred and seventy-four, shall be under the charge and control of four commissioners, who shall perform all the duties and exercise all the powers now by law conferred or imposed upon the police department of the city of New York.

Police force

SEC. 40. The police force shall be appointed by said board, and shall be composed of a superintendent and three inspectors, and as many captains of police, sergeants of police, patrolmen and doormen of police, and as many clerks and employees of police as the Board of police may, from time to time, determine and the funds appropriated allow, except that the number of patrolmen shall not be

* See Appendix, F, and sec. 1, chap. 755, Laws of 1873.

increased in any one year more than one hundred beyond the number authorized the previous year. The Board of police may appoint not exceeding twenty-two surgeons of police, one of whom shall be designated as chief surgeon. They shall detail from the force, to be under direction of the mayor, not exceeding six patrolmen. Police surgeons.

SEC. 41. The government and discipline of the police department shall be such as the Board may, from time to time, by rules and regulations, prescribe, but members of the police force shall be removable only after written charges shall have been preferred against them, and after the charges have been publicly examined into, upon such reasonable notice to the person charged, and in such manner of examination as the rules and regulations of the board of police may prescribe. The clerks and employees shall, except as herein otherwise provided, be appointed and removed at pleasure by the board of police, according to fixed rules to be established by the board. Government and discipline. Clerks.

SEC. 42. The board of police may, by resolution adopted by the unanimous vote of a full board, setting forth the reasons therefor under such rule, retire from office, in such police department or force, any inspector, captain, sergeant, patrolman or surgeon (if disabled while in the actual performance of duty), and place the person so retired upon the pension-roll of the police life insurance fund, and allow him an annual retiring pension not exceeding in amount one-third the annual salary or compensation of such office. But no such inspector, captain, Retired list on pension.

sergeant, surgeon or patrolman shall be so retired from office and placed on the pension-roll except at his own request in writing, unless due notice is given him of the intention so to retire; nor unless it shall be certified to the board by two of the police surgeons that he is, in their opinion, permanently, mentally, or physically incapacitated from duty as such inspector, captain, sergeant, surgeon, or patrolman; nor unless the said board shall concur in such opinion; nor unless the nature and origin of such incapacity shall be stated in the resolution so retiring him.

Present force and pay continued.

SEC. 43. Every person connected with the police department of the city of New York, at the time this act shall take effect, and except as otherwise herein ordered, shall continue in office, and the amount of salary or compensation now legally paid to such person, except as herein otherwise provided or authorized, shall be the salary and compensation fixed for his office under this act; but the commissioners to be appointed under this act may fix the salary and compensation of such clerks other than policemen whom they may be authorized by law to employ.

Qualifications for membership.

SEC. 44. No person shall ever be appointed to membership in the police force, or to continue to hold membership therein, who is not a citizen of the United States, or who has ever been convicted of crime, or who cannot read and write understandingly in the English language, or who shall not have resided within the city and state one year, but skilled officers of experience may be appointed for detective duty who have not resided as herein required. The name, residence, and occupation of each applicant for appointment to any position in the police department, as well as the name, residence, and occupation of each person appointed to any position, shall be published, and such publication shall, in every instance, be made on the Saturday next succeeding such application or appointment, in the City Record. Appointments to be published.

SEC. 45. The board of police may, upon an emergency or apprehension of riot, tumult, mob, insurrection, pestilence, or invasion, appoint as many special patrolmen without pay from among the citizens as it may deem desirable. The board of police, with the approbation in writing of the mayor, or, in case of their disagreement, the governor may, under similar circumstances, demand the assistance of the military of the first division, or of any brigade, regiment, or company thereof, by order in writing, served upon the commanding officer of such division, and such commanding officer shall obey such order. Special patrolmen. Military assistance.

SEC. 46. During the service of any special patrolman authorized as aforesaid, he shall possess all the powers and privileges, and perform all the duties that may be by orders, rules, and regulations from time to time prescribed. Every such special patrolman shall wear a badge, to be prescribed and furnished by the board of police. Powers of special patrolmen.

Resignations

SEC. 47. No member of the police force, under penalty of forfeiting the salary or pay which may be due him, shall withdraw or resign, except by permission of the board of police. Unexplained absence, without leave, of any member of the police force, for five days, shall be deemed and held to be a resignation of such member, and accepted as such.

Police board may issue subpœnas, examine witnesses, etc.

SEC. 48. The board of police shall have power to issue subpœnas, tested in the name of its president, to compel the attendance of witnesses upon any proceedings authorized by its rules and regulations. Each commissioner of police, the superintendent thereof, and the chief clerk and deputy thereof, are hereby authorized and empowered to administer affirmations and oaths to any person summoned and appearing in any matter or proceeding, authorized as aforesaid, and in all matters pertaining to the department or the duties of any officer, or to take any depositions necessary to be made under the orders, rules, and regulations of the board of police, or for the purposes of this act. Any person making a complaint that a felony or misdemeanor has been committed may be required to make affirmation or oath thereto, and for this purpose the inspectors, captains, and sergeants of police shall have power to administer affirmations and oaths. Any willful or corrupt false swearing, by any witness or person, to any material fact in any necessary proceeding under the said orders, rules, and regulations, or under this act, shall be deemed perjury, and punished in the

False swearing.

manner now prescribed by law for such offense. The provisions and procedure of chapter thirty-nine of the laws of eighteen hundred and sixty, passed February eighteen, eighteen hundred and sixty, are hereby applied to the case of any witness subpœnaed under this section.

Station-houses.

SEC. 49. The board of police may, with the authority and approval of the mayor and the common council, from time to time, but with special reference to locating the same as centrally in precincts as possible, establish, provide, and furnish stations and station-houses, or sub-stations and sub-station-houses, at least one to each precinct, for the accommodation thereat of members of the police force, and as places of temporary detention for persons arrested and property taken within the precinct; and shall also provide and furnish such business accommodations, apparatus and articles, and provide for the care thereof, as shall be necessary for the department of police and the transaction of the business of the police department. And the money required for such purposes, and all other sums required for the police department, shall be estimated for and raised in the manner in this act provided generally for the estimating and raising of the necessary funds for the carrying on of the work of the several departments of the city government; and such amounts as may be required from time to time by the said department shall be paid by the comptroller of said city, on the requisition of the treasurer of said department, as ordered by the board thereof, but in such sums and ac-

Police funds, how raised.

cording to such modes and forms as shall be prescribed by the finance department, under the provision of law creating the same.

Rules and regulations.

SEC. 50. The board of police are empowered, in their discretion, to enact, modify and repeal, from time to time, orders, rules and regulations of general discipline of the subordinates under their control, but in strict conformity to the provisions of this act.

Powers of police.

SEC. 51. The members of the police force shall possess in the city of New York, and in every part of this state, all the common law and statutory powers of constables, except for the service of civil process, and any warrant for search or arrest, issued by any magistrate of this state, may be executed, in any part thereof, by any member of the police force, and all the provisions of sections seven, eight and nine of chapter two, title two, part four of the revised statutes, in relation to the giving and taking of bail, shall apply to this act.

Arrests to be taken at once before nearest magistrate, or station-house.

SEC. 52. Each member of the police force, under the penalty of ten days' fine, or dismissal from the force, at the discretion of the board, shall, immediately upon an arrest, convey in person the offender before the nearest sitting magistrate, that he may be dealt with according to law. If the arrest is made during the hours that the magistrate does not regularly hold court, or if the magistrate is not holding court, such offender may be detained in a station-house or precinct thereof, until the next regular public sitting of the magistrate, and no longer, and shall then be conveyed without delay before the magistrate, to be dealt with according to law. And it shall be the duty of the said board, from time to time, to provide suitable rules and regulations to prevent the undue detention of persons arrested, which rules and regulations shall be as operative and binding as if herein specially enacted, subject, however, to the order of the court committing the person arrested.

Undue detention.

SEC. 53. No person holding office under this department shall be liable to military or jury duty, and no officer or patrolman, while actually on duty, shall be liable to arrest on civil process, or to service of subpœna from civil courts.

Exemption from jury and military duty.

SEC. 54. The board of police shall provide suitable accommodations for the detention of witnesses who are unable to furnish security for their appearance in criminal proceedings, to be called the house for the detention of witnesses; and such accommodation shall be in premises other than those employed for the confinement of persons charged with crime, fraud, or disorderly conduct, and be in command of a sergeant of police. And it shall be the duty of all magistrates, when committing witnesses in default of bail, to commit them to such house of detention of witnesses now or hereafter to be used for such purpose.

House of detention for witnesses.

SEC. 55. The board of police shall have power in its

Dismissals.

discretion, on the conviction of a member of the force of any legal offense or neglect of duty, or violation of rules, or neglect or disobedience of orders, or absence without leave, or any conduct injurious to the public peace or welfare, or immoral conduct, or conduct unbecoming an officer, or other breach of discipline, to punish the offending party by reprimand, forfeiting and withholding pay for a specified time, or dismissal from the force; but no more than thirty days' pay shall be forfeited for any offense. All such fines shall be paid forthwith to the treasurer of the department to the account of the police life insurance fund.

Fines.

Official appointment.

SEC. 56. Every member of the police force shall have issued to him by the board of police, a proper warrant of appointment, signed by the president of the said board, and chief clerk or first deputy, which warrant shall contain the date of his appointment and his rank.

Official oath.

SEC. 57. Each member of the police force shall, before entering upon the duties of his office, take an oath of office, and subscribe the same before any officer of the police department who is empowered to administer an oath. The treasurer of the board of police shall give a bond, with two sureties, in the sum of twenty thousand dollars each, for the faithful performance of his duties; said bond to be approved by the comptroller and filed in his office.

Treasurer to give bond.

SEC. 58. It shall be the duty of the superintendent of

police to detail, on each day of election, at least two patrolmen to each election poll.

Policemen detailed at election polls.

Sec. 59. It shall be the duty of the police force, or any member thereof, to prevent any booth, or box, or structure for the distribution of tickets at any election from being erected or maintained within one hundred and fifty feet of any polling place within the city, and to summarily remove any such booth, box or structure, or close and prevent the use thereof.

Election booths.

Sec. 60. The duties of the police surgeons, and the extent and bounds of their districts, shall be assigned from time to time by the rules and regulations of the board of police.

Police surgeons.

Sec. 61. All property or money alleged or supposed to have been feloniously obtained, or which shall be lost or abandoned, and which shall be hereafter taken into the custody of any member of the police force, or criminal court of the city of New York, or which shall come into the custody of any police justice, shall be, by such member or justice, or by order of said court, given into the custody of and kept by the property clerk of the police, and all such property and money shall be particularly registered by said property clerk in a book kept for that purpose, which shall contain the name of the owner, if ascertained, the place where found, the name of the person from whom taken, with the general circumstances, the date of its receipt, the name of the officer recovering

Stolen property to be in charge of property-clerk.

the same, the names of all claimants thereto, and any final disposition of such property or money.

Property, how returned. SEC. 62. Whenever property or money shall be taken from persons arrested, and shall be alleged to have been feloniously obtained, or to be the proceeds of crime, and whenever so brought, with such claimant and the person arrested, before some magistrate for adjudication, and the magistrate shall be then and there satisfied from evidence that the person arrested is innocent of the offense alleged, and that the property rightfully belongs to him, then said magistrate may thereupon, in writing, order such property or money to be returned, and the property clerk, if he have it, to deliver such property or money to the accused person himself, and not to any attorney, agent or clerk of such accused person.

Claims for property to be made on oath. SEC. 63. If any claim to the ownership of such property or money shall be made on oath before the magistrate, by or in behalf of any other persons than the person arrested, and the said accused person shall be held for trial or examination, such property or money shall remain in the custody of the property clerk until the discharge or conviction of the person accused.

Lost property to be advertised in City Record. SEC. 64. All property or money taken on suspicion of having been feloniously obtained, or of being the proceeds of crime, and for which there is no other claimant than the person from whom such property was taken, and all lost property coming into the possession of any member of the said police force, and all property and money taken from pawnbrokers as the proceeds of crime, or by any such member from persons supposed to be insane, intoxicated or otherwise incapable of taking care of themselves, shall be transmitted, as soon as practicable, to the property clerk, to be registered and advertised in the City Record for the benefit of all persons interested, and for the information of the public, as to the amount and disposition of the property so taken into custody by the police.

When detained property shall be sold.

SEC. 65. All property and money that shall remain in the custody of the property clerk for the period of six months without any lawful claimant thereto, after having been advertised in the City Record for the period of ten days, shall be sold at public auction in a suitable room to be designated for such purpose, and the proceeds of such sale shall be paid into the police life insurance fund.

When property or articles may be used in court.

SEC. 66. If any property or money placed in the custody of the property clerk shall be desired as evidence in any police or other criminal court, such property shall be delivered to any officer who shall present an order to that effect from such court. Such property, however, shall not be retained in said court, but shall be returned to such property clerk, to be disposed of according to the previous provisions of this act.

Powers conferred on police board.

SEC. 67. The board of police by this act created shall possess all the powers conferred upon the existing board of police by chapter six hundred and seventy-seven of the laws of eighteen hundred and seventy-two, and any act or acts amendatory thereof or supplemental thereto, except as herein otherwise provided; and shall establish in their department a bureau, which shall be called the bureau of street cleaning; the chief officer of which shall be a police officer and shall be called "inspector of street cleaning;" and who shall, under the supervision of the board of police, have charge of the cleaning of the streets, avenues and public places of the city. He shall supervise and enforce the performance of the conditions of any existing contract for such cleaning, or for the removal, under any contract now existing or hereafter made by the board of health, of night soil and contents of sinks and privies, and offal and dead animals; and shall perform such additional cleaning as, in the opinion of the board of health, is necessary to keep said streets, avenues and public places clean. He shall possess all the powers and rights imposed upon or reserved to the city inspector in any law or ordinance, or in any contract now in force, so far as the same relates to street cleaning. He shall file with the comptroller monthly a statement, under oath, showing the number of persons, and at what salary or compensation, that were employed during each day in the preceding month, and shall keep and preserve regular pay-rolls, which shall be open to reasonable public inspection.

Shall establish a bureau of street cleaning.

Inspector on street cleaning.

Absence or illness of superintendent.

SEC. 68. In case of the disability, absence or illness of the superintendent of police, the commissioners of police may, by resolution, designate such officer of the police force as they may choose to execute and perform the duties of the superintendent during the period of such disability, absence or illness.

SEC. 69. The police department is hereby authorized and empowered, in its name or in the name of its president or treasurer, to take and prosecute any appropriate action or proceeding in any court of record, or to continue any action heretofore commenced for such purpose, which the board of police of the metropolitan police district or its treasurer, or any other public officer or officers, but for the passage of said act, and of any other act passed since the first of January, eighteen hundred and seventy, could have taken and prosecuted, to compel the county of Richmond, or the board of supervisors of that county, or any officer of that county, to make payment of the sums due from and owing by said county of Richmond, by reason of the failure of said county and its officers to pay to the said board of metropolitan police, or the treasurer of said board of police, or into the treasury of the state, the moneys required to pay the salaries and compensation of the members of the police force of the metropolitan police district doing duty in the said county of Richmond, and defray the other lawful expenses of said police force, chargeable upon the said county of Richmond, as specified in the annual financial estimates heretofore made by the said board of metropolitan police, and all moneys that may be so collected shall

Police funds due from county of Richmond.

be paid to the chamberlain of the city of New York; the moneys so due and owing having been advanced, by the said board of metropolitan police, out of moneys raised in and contributed to the metropolitan police fund by the county of New York.

ARTICLE VIII.

Of the Department of Public Works.

Commissioner. SEC. 70. There shall be a department of public works, the head or chief officer of which shall be called "commissioner of public works," who shall hold office for four years, and until his successor is appointed, unless sooner removed, as herein provided. Whenever the words "street commissioner" shall occur in any existing law, ordinance, resolution, contract or document, it shall be deemed to mean the aforesaid commissioner of public works, and whenever in any law, or in any ordinance of the corporation, the words "street department" shall occur, it shall be deemed and construed hereafter to mean the department of public works and the commissioner thereof. Deputy. The commissioner of public works may appoint a deputy commissioner of public works, who shall, in addition to his other powers, possess every power and perform all and every duty belonging to the office of said commissioner, whenever so empowered by said commissioner by written authority, designating therein a period of time not extending beyond the period of three months, nor beyond the term of office of the said commissioner of public works, during which said power and duty may be exercised; and such designation and authority shall be duly filed in and remain on record in the department of public works. The said deputy commissioner of public works shall possess the like authority in the case of the absence or disability of the commissioner of public works. And it shall be the duty of the commissioner to remove all obstructions now existing, or which may hereafter be placed upon any street or sidewalk, or public ground not inclosed in any public park; provided, however, that nothing contained in this section shall affect or prevent the continuance of any proceedings already commenced for assessing the expense of executing any contract made by the department of public works or the commissioner thereof.

Powers of deputy.

Powers of commissioner.

SEC. 71. The said department shall have cognizance and control—

1. Of all structures and property connected with the supply and distribution of Croton water.

2. Of the collection of the revenues arising from the sale or use of the Croton water.

3. Of opening, altering, regulating, grading, flagging, curbing, guttering, and lighting streets, roads, places and avenues.

4. Of repairing and construction of public roads.

5. Of the care of public buildings.

6. Of the filling of sunken lots.

7. Of public sewers and drainage.

8. Of street vaults and openings in sidewalks.

9. Of paving, repairing and repaving streets, and keeping the same clear of obstructions.*

10. Of digging and constructing wells.

Bureaus. SEC. 72. There shall be eight bureaus in the department of public works:

Water purveyor. 1. A bureau for laying water-pipes, and the construction and repair of sewers, wells and hydrants, paving and repaving and repairing streets, the chief officer of which shall be called "water purveyor."

Water register. 2. A bureau for the collection of revenue derived from the sale and use of water; the chief officer of which shall be called "water register."

Chief engineer. 3. A bureau having care of all structures and property connected with the supply and distribution of Croton water; the chief officer of which shall be called "chief engineer of the Croton aqueduct," with power to appoint and remove at pleasure, and detail a staff of assistant engineers. He and they must be civil engineers of at least ten years' experience. The commissioner may delegate to this bureau any power and duty now conferred by

* See Appendix, G.

law or ordinance on the chief engineer of the Croton aqueduct board.

4. A bureau for grading, flagging, curbing and guttering streets; the chief officer of which shall be called "superintendent of street improvements." Superintendent of street improvements.

5. A bureau of lamps and gas; the chief officer of which shall be called "superintendent of lamps and gas." Superintendent of lamps and gas.

6. A bureau of streets and roads; the chief officer of which shall be called "superintendent of streets." Superintendent of streets.

7. A bureau of repairs and supplies, which shall have cognizance of all supplies and repairs to public buildings, works, lands, and places, and all other repairs and supplies not provided for in other departments; the chief officer of which shall be called "superintendent of repairs and supplies," and shall be a practical builder. Superintendent of repairs and supplies.

8. A bureau for the removal of incumbrances on the streets or sidewalks; the chief officer of which shall be called the "superintendent of incumbrances," to whom all complaints shall be made, and by whom such incumbrances shall be removed. Superintendent of incumbrances.

SEC. 73. The commissioner of public works, in conjunction with the mayor and comptroller, is authorized from time to time to contract, as provided in section ninety-[one] of this act, for lighting the streets, avenues and places of the city with gas, but shall not make any arrangement or agreement with any company or com- Contract for lighting streets.

panies for such purpose for a period longer than one year at any given time, nor for an amount in excess of the amount appropriated therefor. The commissioner of public works is hereby authorized, in his discretion, to cause water meters, the pattern and price of which shall be approved by the mayor, comptroller, and chief engineer of the Croton aqueduct, to be placed in all stores, workshops, hotels, manufactories, public edifices, at wharves, ferry-houses, stables, and in all places in which water is furnished for business consumption by the department of public works, except private dwellings, so that all water so furnished therein or thereat may be measured and known by the said department, and for the purpose of ascertaining the ratable portion which consumers of water should pay for the water therein or thereat received and used. Thereafter, as shall be determined by the commissioner of public works, the said department shall make out all bills and charges for water furnished by them to each and every consumer as aforesaid, to whose consumption a meter as aforesaid is affixed, in ratable proportion to the water consumed, as ascertained by the meter on his or her premises or places occupied or used as aforesaid. All expenses of meters, their connections and setting, water rates, and other lawful charges for the supply of Croton water, shall be a lien upon the premises where such water is supplied as now provided by law. Nothing herein contained shall be construed so as to remit or prevent the due collection of arrearages or charges for water consumption heretofore incurred, nor

Water meters.

Water bills.

Meters a lien on premises.

interfere with the proper liens therefor, nor of charges or rates, or liens hereafter to be incurred for water consumption in any dwelling-house, building or place which may not contain one of the meters aforesaid. The department of public works hereby created shall have and possess all the powers and functions heretofore or now possessed by the department of public parks, or the department of public works, in relation to the construction of the boulevard (road or public drive), streets, avenues, and roads above Fifty-ninth street, not embraced within the limits of or immediately adjacent to any park or public place; and all provisions of law conferring powers, and devolving duties upon the department of public parks, in relation thereto, are hereby transferred to and conferred upon the said department of public works.

To possess certain powers of department of parks.

ARTICLE IX.

Of the Department of Public Charities and Correction.

Board of charities and correction.

SEC. 74. The department of public charities and correction shall hereafter be composed of and have for its head a board of three persons, which board shall possess all the powers and discharge all the duties now conferred upon such department by special laws and by all the provisions of chapter five hundred and ten of the laws of eighteen hundred and sixty, and the acts and parts of acts amendatory thereof, except as the same are modified or repealed by the provisions of this act. The commission-

Their term of office.

ers, except those first appointed, shall hold office for six years, unless sooner removed as herein provided. There shall be under said commissioners a bureau of charities and a bureau of correction. The bureau of charities shall have charge of all matters relating to persons not criminals. The bureau of correction shall have charge of all matters relating to criminals.

Bureaus.

Moneys, how used.

SEC. 75. [*As amended by sec.* 10, *chap.* 757, *laws of* 1873.] No money belonging to the city, or city and county of New York, raised by taxation upon the property of the citizens thereof, shall be appropriated in aid of any religious or denominational school, neither shall any property, real or personal, belonging to said city, or said city and county, be disposed of to any such school, except upon the sale thereof at public auction, after the same has been duly advertised, at which sale such school shall be the highest bidder, and upon payment of the sum so bid into the city treasury, neither shall any property belonging to the city, or city and county, be leased to any school under the control of any religious or denominational institution, except upon such terms as city property may be leased to private parties after the same has been duly advertised.

ARTICLE X.

Of the Fire Department.*

SEC. 76. The fire department shall have for its head a board, to consist of three persons to be known as fire commissioners of the city of New York, who, except those first appointed, shall hold their offices for six years, unless sooner removed as herein provided. There shall be in this department three bureaus. One bureau shall be charged with the duty of preventing and extinguishing fires and of protecting property from water used at fires, the principal officer of which shall be called the "chief of department." Another bureau shall be charged with the execution of all laws relating to the storage, sale and use of combustible materials, the principal officer of which shall be called "inspector of combustibles." Another bureau shall be charged with the investigation of the origin and cause of fires, the principal officer of which shall be called "fire marshal." The fire marshal shall possess all the powers and perform all the duties now possessed and performed by the fire marshal, and appointed pursuant to chapter three hundred and eighty-three of the laws of eighteen hundred and seventy, and chapter five hundred and eighty-four of the laws of eighteen hundred and seventy-one, and the acts amendatory or supplementary thereof. Such fire marshal and his assistants shall hereafter be appointed by the board of

Fire commissioners.

Bureaus.

Fire marshal.

* See Appendix, H.

fire commissioners, who shall possess all the powers with reference thereto conferred by said acts upon the board of police.

Discipline, rules, orders, etc.

SEC. 77. The government and discipline of the fire department shall be such as the board may from time to time by rules, regulations, and orders prescribe; but officers and members of the uniformed force shall be removable only after written charges shall have been preferred against them, and after the charges have been publicly examined into, upon such reasonable notice to the person charged, and in such manner of examination as the rules and regulations of the board of commissioners may prescribe. Sections forty-eight, fifty, fifty-one fifty-five, fifty-eight, sixty, sixty-one, sixty-two, of chapter one hundred and thirty-seven of the laws of eighteen hundred and seventy, are hereby made applicable to the fire department and its subordinates, so far as the same are pertinent, in the same manner as if the same were therein named.

Fines.

Any and all fines collected from subordinates shall be deposited in "the fire department relief fund" created by chapter seven hundred and forty-two of the laws of eighteen hundred and seventy-one, and the treasurer of said fund shall give a bond, with one or more sureties, in the sum of twenty thousand dollars for the faithful performance of his duties; said bond to be approved by the comptroller and filed in his office.

Membership.

SEC. 78. [*As amended by sec.* 11, *chap.* 757, *laws of* 1873.] No person shall ever be appointed to membership in the fire department, or continue to hold membership therein, who is not a citizen of the United States, or who has ever been convicted of crime, or who cannot read and write understandingly in the English language, or who shall not have resided within the state one year.

SEC. 79. The board of commissioners by this act created shall possess and exercise all the powers and perform all the duties conferred and prescribed by chapter two hundred and forty-nine of the laws of eighteen hundred and sixty-five, and any act or acts amendatory thereof or supplementary thereto, not inconsistent with the provisions of this act, and except as herein otherwise provided. General powers of board.

ARTICLE XI.

Of the Health Department.*

SEC. 80. The Health Department shall consist of the president of the board of police, the health officer of the port, and two officers to be called "commissioners of health," one of whom shall have been a pratising physician for not less than five years preceding his appointment. The commissioner of health, who is not a physician, shall be the president of the board, and shall be so designated in his appointment. These several officers shall together constitute a board, which shall be Board of health.

* See Appendix, I.

the head of the health department. The commissioners of health, except those first appointed, shall hold their offices for six years, unless sooner removed as herein provided.

Bureaus. SEC. 81. There shall be two bureaus in this department. The chief officer of one bureau shall be called the "sanitary superintendent," who, at the time of his appointment, shall have been, for at least ten years, a practising physician and for three years a resident of the city of New York, and he shall be the chief executive officer of said department. The chief officer of the second bureau shall be called the "register of records;" and in said bureau shall be recorded, without fees, every birth, marriage and death, and all inquisitions of coroners which shall occur or be taken within the city of New York. But in cases of inquests, where the jury shall find that death was caused by negligence or malicious injury, only a copy of the record need be filed in said bureau. Said board may, with the consent of the board of police, impose any portion of the duties of subordinates in said department upon subordinates in the police department and may delegate any portion of its powers to the president or sanitary superintendent, to be exercised when the board is not in session. The said board of health may appoint an attorney at a salary not exceeding two thousand five hundred dollars a year, to be provided for and paid as other salaries in said department.

Record of birth, etc.

Board may appoint attorney.

Sanitary code. SEC. 82. It shall be the duty of said board, immediately upon organization under this act, to cause to be conformed to this article the sanitary ordinances then or lately adopted by the existing department of health, which shall be called the "sanitary code." And said health department is hereby authorized and empowered to add to such sanitary code, from time to time, and shall publish additional provisions for the security of life and health in the city of New York, and therein to distribute appropriate powers and duties to the members and employees of the board of health, which shall be published in the City Record. Any violation of said code shall be treated and punished as a misdemeanor, and the offender shall also be liable to pay a penalty of fifty dollars, to be recovered in a civil action in the name of the mayor, aldermen, and commonalty of the city of New York. All orders duly made by the existing department of health, and by their terms or necessary legal effect to be executed in the city of New York, may be executed, and the execution thereof compelled, and the execution of such of them as are partly executed may be compelled by the department of health hereby created; and the said orders may be severally rescinded or modified by last said department, with like effect as could have been done by the existing department of health at the time the said orders were severally made. The said department may discharge all liens upon real estate in the city of New York, created in proceedings instituted by the metropolitan board of health, or the existing department of health, in the same manner and for the same causes that, by laws existing January first,

Penalty for violations.

Liens.

eighteen hundred and seventy, they could be discharged by the metropolitan board of health.

Powers of former acts merged in board.

[*Amended by adding the following—sec.* 12, *chap.* 757, *laws of* 1873.] The authority, duty and powers conferred or enjoined upon the metropolitan board of health by chapter seventy-four of the laws of eighteen hundred and sixty-six, and the several acts amendatory thereof, and by any other subsequent laws of this state, and, upon the several officers and members of said board, not inconsistent with the provisions of this act, are hereby conferred upon and vested in, or enjoined upon, and shall hereafter be exclusively exercised in the city of New York, by the health department and board of health created by this act; and by the officers of the said board of health and the said health department; and the same are to be exercised in the manner specified in the said chapter seventy-four, of the laws of eighteen hundred and sixty-six, and the several acts amendatory thereof, and by any other subsequent laws of the state, and in conformity to the provisions of this act.

ARTICLE XII.

Of the Department of Public Parks.*

Commissioners of parks.

SEC. 83. [*As amended by sec.* 13, *chap.* 757, *laws of* 1873.] The department of public parks shall

* See Appendix, F, sec. 2.

control and manage all public parks and streets immediately adjoining the same above Fifty-ninth street, and public places which are the realty of the city of New York, except the buildings in the city hall park, and save as herein otherwise provided; and shall have all the powers and duties belonging to the department or commissioners of parks not inconsistent with the provisions of this act, and the laying out and preparing maps and plans of all streets, avenues and drives above Fifty-ninth street. **Powers.**

SEC. 84. [*As amended by sec.* 2, *chap.* 300, *laws of* 1874.] This department shall be under the charge of a board to consist of four members, who, except those first appointed, shall hold their offices for five years, unless sooner removed as herein provided. The office of the commissioner of parks, whose term of office expires on the first day of May, eighteen hundred and seventy-four, is hereby abolished on and after said date. The department of public parks, on and after the first day of May, eighteen hundred and seventy-four, shall be under the charge and control of four commissioners, who shall perform all the duties and exercise all the powers now by law conferred or imposed upon the department of public parks of the city of New York. **Organization of board.** **Board to consist of four commissioners.**

ARTICLE XIII.

Of the Department of Buildings.*

Superintendent of buildings.

SEC. 85. [*As amended by sec.* 15, *chap.* 757, *laws of* 1873.] There shall be a department called the department of buildings, which shall be under the control of an officer, who shall be known as the superintendent of buildings, and shall be the same person nominated as commissioner of buildings by the mayor of the city of New York on the fifteenth day of May, one thousand eight hundred and seventy-three, and confirmed by the board of aldermen of said city on the sixteenth day of May, one thousand eight hundred and seventy-three, which said superintendent shall hold office for the full term for which said commissioner was appointed, unless sooner removed, as provided by law for the removal of heads of departments.

Powers and duties continued.

SEC. 86. [*As amended by sec.* 15, *chap.* 757, *laws of* 1873.] Each and all the powers and duties of said department and all its officers and employees, and subordinates, and their qualifications shall continue, and be exercised as now authorized by special laws in relation to buildings in the city of New York; and it shall not be lawful for any officer or employee in said department to be engaged in conducting or

* See Appendix, J.

carrying on business as an architect, carpenter, mason, or builder, while holding office in said department.

ARTICLE XIV.

The Department of Taxes and Assessments.

SEC. 87. The department of taxes and assessments shall have for its head a president, who shall be so designated in his appointment, and two commissioners, who together shall possess all the powers and perform all the duties now possessed and performed by the commissioners of taxes and assessments. Except that it shall require a majority of such commissioners to correct or reduce the assessed valuation of the personal property of any person, and that no tax or personal property shall be remitted, canceled, or reduced, unless the applicant or party aggrieved shall satisfy the commissioners that he has been prevented by absence from the city or by illness from making his complaint or application to them within the time allowed by law for the correction of taxes. They may regulate and abolish the subordinate offices and bureaus, as shall seem most advantageous to the public service. They shall, except those first appointed, hold their offices for six years, unless sooner removed as herein provided.

Commissioners of taxes and assessments.

Remission of taxes.

Term of office.

ARTICLE XV.

Of the Department of Docks.

Department of docks.

SEC. 88. There shall be a department of docks, the head of which shall be a board consisting of three persons residing in the city of New York, who, except those first appointed, shall hold office for the term of six years, unless sooner removed as herein provided, and shall possess such powers and perform such duties as are now possessed by the existing department of docks, but said board shall not have the power to change the exterior line of piers and bulk-heads in the city of New York as now established by law.

Exterior line.

ARTICLE XVI.

General Provisions, Powers, and Limitations.

Quorum.

SEC. 89. A majority of the members of a board in any department of the city government, and also of the board for the revision and correction of assessments, shall constitute a quorum to fully perform and discharge any act or duty authorized, possessed by, or imposed upon any department or any board aforesaid, and with the same legal effect as if every member of any such board aforesaid had been present, except as herein otherwise specially provided. Each board may, except as herein otherwise provided, choose, in its own pleasure, one of its members, who shall be its president, and one who shall be

Officers.

its treasurer, and may appoint a chief clerk or secretary. No expense shall be incurred by any of the departments, boards, or officers thereof, unless an appropriation shall have been previously made covering such expense.

How expenses may be incurred.

SEC. 90. Whatever provisions and regulations, other than those herein specially authorized, may become requisite for the fuller organization, perfecting, and carrying out of the powers and duties prescribed to any department by this act, shall be provided for by ordinance of the common council, who are hereby authorized to enact such necessary ordinances. And it shall be the duty of the common council to provide for the accountability of all officers and other persons, save as herein otherwise provided, to whom the receipt or expenditure of the funds of the city shall be intrusted, by requiring from them sufficient security for the performance of their duties or trust, which security shall be annually renewed; but the security first taken shall remain in force until new security shall be given.

Full powers given to common council.

Officers intrusted with funds to give security.

SEC. 91. All contracts to be made or let for work to be done, or supplies to be furnished, except as herein otherwise provided, and all sales of personal property in the custody of the several departments or bureaus, shall be made by the appropriate heads of departments under such regulations as now exist or shall be established by ordinances of the common council. Whenever any work is necessary to be done to complete or perfect a particular job, or any supply is needful for any particular purpose,

Contracts.

Work to be done under contracts.

which work and job is to be undertaken or supply furnished for the corporation, and the several parts of the said work or supply shall together involve the expenditure of more than one thousand dollars, the same shall be by contract, under such regulations concerning it as shall be established by ordinance of the common council, excepting such works now in progress as are authorized by law or ordinance to be done otherwise than by contract; and unless otherwise ordered by a vote of three-fourths of the members elected to the common council; and all contracts shall be entered into by the appropriate heads of departments, and shall, except as herein otherwise provided, be founded on sealed bids or proposals, made in compliance with public notice duly advertised in the City Record, said notice to be published at least ten days; and all such contracts, when given, shall be given to the lowest bidder, the terms of whose contracts shall be settled by the counsel to the corporation as an act of preliminary specification to the bid or proposal, and who shall give security for the faithful performance of his contract in the manner prescribed and required by ordinance; and the adequacy and sufficiency of this security shall, in addition to the justification and acknowledgment, be approved by the comptroller. All bids or proposals shall be publicly opened by the officers advertising for the same and in the presence of the comptroller, but the opening of the bids shall not be postponed if the comptroller shall, after due notice, fail to attend. If the lowest bidder shall neglect or refuse to accept to contract within forty-eight hours

Proposals to be advertised.

Contractor to give security.

Bids to be publicly opened.

Neglect to ratify an accepted bid.

after written notice that the same has been awarded to his bid or proposal, or if he accepts but does not execute the contract and give the proper security, it shall be re-advertised and relet as above provided. In case any work shall be abandoned by any contractor, it shall be re-advertised and relet by the head of the appropriate department, in the manner in this section provided.

SEC. 92. All property sold shall be sold at auction, after previous public notice, under the superintendence of the appropriate head of department. Every contract, when made and entered into, as before provided for, shall be executed in duplicate, and shall be filed in the department of finance; a receipt for each payment, made on account of or in satisfaction of the same, shall be indorsed on the said contract by the party receiving the warrant, which warrant shall be only given to the person interested in such contract, or his authorized representative. The proceeds of all sales made under and by virtue of this act shall, except as provided in section sixty-five hereof, be by the officer receiving the same immediately deposited with the chamberlain; and the account of sales, verified by the officer making the sales, shall be immediately filed in the office of the comptroller. No expenditure for work or supplies involving an amount for which no contract is required shall be made, except the necessity therefor be certified to by the head of the appropriate department, and the expenditure has been duly authorized and appropriated.

Property to be sold at auction.

Contracts to be filed in duplicate.

Proceeds of sales.

Certificate of office.

SEC. 93. Every person who shall be appointed or elected to any office under this act shall receive a certificate of appointment, designating the term for which such person has been appointed or elected.

Oath to be taken by all officers.

SEC. 94. Every person elected or appointed to any office under the city government shall, within five days after notice of such election or appointment, take and subscribe, before the mayor, or any judge of a court of record, an oath or affirmation faithfully to perform the duties of his office; which oath or affirmation shall be filed in the office of the mayor.

Violations of this act, how punished.

SEC. 95. Any officer of the city government, or person employed in its service, who shall willfully violate or evade any of the provisions of this act, or commit any fraud upon the city, or convert any of the public property to his own use, or knowingly permit any other person so to convert it, or by gross or culpable neglect of duty allow the same to be lost to the city, shall be deemed guilty of a misdemeanor, and, in addition to the penalties imposed by law, and on conviction, shall forfeit his office, and be excluded forever after from receiving or holding any office under the city government; and any person who shall willfully swear falsely in any oath or affirmation required by this act shall be guilty of perjury.

Salary in lieu of fees, perquisites, etc.

SEC. 96. [*As amended by sec.* 16, *chap.* 757, *laws of* 1873.] No officer of the city government, except the city marshals, shall have or receive to his own use any fees, perquisites, or commissions, or any percentage; but every such officer shall be paid by a fixed salary, and all fees, percentages and commissions received by any such officer shall be the property of the city. And every officer who shall receive any fees, perquisites, commissions, percentages or other money which should be paid over to the city, shall, before he shall be entitled to receive any salary, make under oath a detailed return to the comptroller, showing the amount of all such fees, commissions, percentages, perquisites and moneys received by him since the last preceding report, the person from whom received, and the reason for its payment, and shall produce the receipt of the chamberlain, showing the payment to him, by said officer, of the aggregate amount thereof. All sums received as above or for licenses or permits shall be paid over weekly, without deduction, by the officers or department receiving them, to the chamberlain, and a detailed return under oath shall at the same time be made in such form as the comptroller shall prescribe, stating when and from whom, and for what use, such moneys were received. But nothing herein contained shall be construed so as to repeal, modify, or otherwise affect the provisions of the fourteenth section of chapter seven hundred and forty-two of the laws of eighteen hundred and seventy-one.

Fees, etc., to be paid over weekly.

Salaries, how fixed.

SEC. 97. The salaries of all officers paid from the city treasury, whose offices now exist but are not embraced in any department, shall be fixed by the board of apportionment. Such board may, by a majority vote, reduce any such salaries, but shall not increase the salary of any office the compensation of which now exceeds three thousand dollars.

When salaries shall be prescribed by ordinance.

SEC. 98. The salaries of all officers, whose offices may be created by the common council for the purpose of giving effect to the provisions of this act, shall be prescribed by ordinance or resolution, to be passed by the common council, and approved as hereinbefore provided for the approval of ordinances or resolutions.

Bidder in arrears.

SEC. 99. No bid shall be accepted from, or contract awarded to, any person who is in arrears to the corporation upon debt or contract, or who is a defaulter, as surety or otherwise, upon any obligation to the corporation.

Bribery, in any form, to be deemed felony.

SEC. 100. Every person who shall promise, offer, or give, or cause, or aid, or abet in causing to be promised, offered, or given, or furnish or agree to furnish, in whole or in part, to any other person, to be promised, offered or given, to any member of the common council, or any officer of the corporation, or clerk, after his election or appointment as such officer, member, or clerk, or before or after he shall have qualified and taken his seat, or entered upon his duty, any moneys, goods, right in action or other property, or anything of value, or any pecuniary advantage, present or prospective, with intent to influence his vote, opinion, judgment or action on any question, matter, cause or proceedings which may be then pending, or may by law be at any time brought before him in his official or clerical capacity, shall be deemed guilty of a felony, and shall, upon conviction, be imprisoned in a penitentiary for a term not exceeding two years, or shall be fined not exceeding five thousand dollars, or both, in the discretion of the court. Every officer in this section enumerated, who shall accept any such gift or promise, or undertaking to make the same under any agreement or understanding that his vote, opinion, judgment or action shall be influenced thereby, or shall be given in any question, matter, cause or proceeding then or at any time pending, or which may by law be brought before him in his official capacity, shall be deemed guilty of a felony, and shall, upon conviction, be disqualified from holding any public office, trust or appointment under the city of New York, and shall forfeit his office, and shall be punished by imprisonment in the penitentiary not exceeding two years, or by a fine not exceeding five thousand dollars, or both, in the discretion of the court. Every person offending against either of the provisions of this section shall be a competent witness against any other person offending in the same transaction, and may be compelled to appear and give evidence before any grand jury, or in any court, in the same manner as other persons; but the testimony so given shall not be used in any prosecution or proceeding, civil or criminal, against the person so testifying.

How punished.

Offenders competent witnesses.

Corporation officers not to be interested in contracts.

SEC. 101. No member of the common council, head of department, chief of bureau, deputy thereof, or clerk therein, or other officer of the corporation, shall be or become, directly or indirectly, interested in or in the performance of any contract, work or business, or the sale of any article, the expense, price or consideration of which is payable from the city treasury, or by any assessment levied by any act or ordinance of the common council; nor in the purchase or lease of any real estate or other property belonging to or taken by the corporation, or which shall be sold for taxes or assessments, or by virtue of legal process at the suit of the said corporation.

Penalty.

If any person in this section mentioned shall, during the time for which he was elected or appointed, knowingly acquire an interest in any contract or work with the city, or any department or officer thereof, unless the same shall be devolved upon him by law, he shall, on conviction thereof, forfeit his office, and be punished as for a misdemeanor.

When contract shall be declared void.

All such contracts in which any such person is or becomes interested shall, at the option of the comptroller, be forfeited and void. No person in this section named shall give or promise to give any portion of his compensation or any money or valuable thing to any officer of the city, or to any other person, in consideration of his having been or being nominated, appointed, elected or employed as such officer, agent, clerk or employee, under the penalty of forfeiting his office and being forever disqualified from being elected, appointed, or employed in the service of the city, and shall, on conviction, be punished for a misdemeanor.

Commissioners of the sinking fund.

SEC. 102. [*As amended by sec.* 17, *chap.* 757, *laws of* 1873.] There shall continue to be, as now provided and recognized by special laws and ordinances, a board of commissioners of the sinking fund composed of the mayor, recorder, chamberlain, comptroller, and the chairman of the finance committee of the board of aldermen, with all the powers and duties now assigned, designated and ratified by existing laws and ordinances. The said board shall have power to sell or lease, for the highest marketable price or rental, at public auction or by sealed bids, and always after public advertisement and appraisal under the direction of said board, any city property, except wharves and piers. But if said property be market property, excepting the market between Sixteenth and Seventeenth streets, east of avenue "C," the market in Gouverneur slip, and the market in Old slip, it shall not be sold or leased unless under a condition that the puschaser or lessee thereof shall maintain said market property as and for the purposes of a public market, for at least ten years from and after such sale or lease, and under due ordinances of the common council or of the department of health, or under stipulations in the deed of sale or lease. The proceeds of said sale or leasing shall, on receipt thereof, after paying necessary

Have power to sell or lease property.

Market property.

Proceeds of sale.

charges, be immediately paid to the credit of the sinking fund. It shall be lawful for the commissioners of the sinking fund of the city of New York, in their discretion, and they are hereby empowered in such discretion to cancel any portion of the indebtedness of the said city held by them, which is by law redeemable from the sinking fund, and to sell any stocks and bonds which they may hold that are not payable from said fund, and with the proceeds of such sale of stocks and bonds to buy any other stocks and bonds which are payable from said fund.

SEC. 103. [*Repealed by sec.* 18, *chap.* 757, *laws of* 1873.]

Election laws, how applied.

SEC. 104. All the provisions of law now in force in regard to the duration, manner of conducting elections, and canvass, estimate and disposition of votes at general elections shall apply to each election of city officers.

Board of street opening, powers of.

SEC. 105. The mayor, comptroller, commissioner of public works, the president of the department of public parks, and the president of the board of aldermen, shall hereafter together form a board to be known as "the board of street opening and improvement," in place and stead of the board of street openings heretofore constituted by law; shall keep full records of its proceedings, and shall have all the powers and authority as to laying out, opening, widening, straightening, extending, altering and closing streets or avenues, or parts of streets or avenues, in that part of the city of New York south of Fifty-ninth street, now in any manner otherwise conferred and vested by any other law or provision thereof, or under existing laws which relate to altering the map or plan of said city; and the said board are hereby authorized and empowered, whenever they may deem it for public interest so to do, after laying its proposed action before the board of aldermen, and publishing full notice of the same for ten days in the City Record herein provided for, to alter the map or plan of New York city so as to lay out new streets in said part of said city, and from time to time to cause maps, showing the several streets or avenues so laid out, opened, widened, straightened, extended, altered or closed by them, to be certified by them and filed, one in the office of the department of public works of said city, and one in the office of the counsel to the corporation of said city, and it shall be the duty of the said counsel to the corporation, on the filing of said maps in his office, together with a requisition in writing of said board, immediately to take proceedings, in the name of the mayor, aldermen and commonalty of said city, to acquire title for the use of the public to the land required for the streets or avenues so laid out, opened, widened, straightened, extended or altered, and for that purpose to make application to the supreme court in the first judicial district, and in such manner as the said board shall direct, for the appointment of commissioners of estimate and assessment, indicating in such application the land required for that purpose by reference to said maps on file as aforesaid; and the pro-

Notices to lay out new streets to be published.

Proceedings to acquire title.

ceedings to acquire title to such lands shall be had pursuant to such acts as shall be then in force relative to the opening, straightening, extending, widening or altering streets, roads, avenues and public squares and places in the city of New York, which said acts, so far as the same are not inconsistent with the provisions of this section, are hereby made applicable to the streets and avenues, or parts of streets and avenues, so laid out, opened, widened, straightened, extended and altered, and to the proceedings authorized hereby, except that the commissioners of estimate and assessment who may be appointed by the supreme court for acquiring title to any land required for the purposes of this section may assess therefor all such lands and tenements as they may deem to be benefited by such improvement, and to the extent and amount which they may deem such lands and tenements benefited thereby; and the said board is also authorized and empowered to close all such streets and avenues, or such parts thereof as they may deem for the public interest so to do, and to direct the said counsel to the corporation to take such proceedings in the name of the mayor, aldermen and commonalty for the closing of such streets or avenues, or parts thereof, as are now or shall be then provided by law, who shall thereupon apply to the supreme court for the appointment of commissioners of estimate and assessment in the matter of the closing of said street, avenue or part thereof in the manner provided by law. And said board is also authorized and empowered to discontinue any and all legal proceedings

Closing of streets.

When legal proceedings as to streets may be discontinued.

taken for laying out, opening, widening, straightening, extending, altering or closing streets or avenues, or parts of streets or avenues, south of Fifty-ninth street, under this act, at any time before the confirmation of the report of the commissioners of estimate and assessment in such proceedings, if in the opinion of said board the public interest requires such discontinuance, and with power to cause new proceedings to be taken in such cases for the appointment of new commissioners. A majority of said board shall constitute a quorum, but the vote of a majority of all the members thereof shall be necessary to any act of said board. The comptroller of the city of New York, is authorized to borrow, from time to time, on the credit of the corporation, in anticipation of its revenues, and not to exceed in amount the amount of such revenues, such sums as may be necessary to meet expenditures under the appropriations for each current year. No action shall be maintained against the mayor, aldermen and commonalty of the city of New York, unless the claim on which the action is brought has been presented to the comptroller, and he has neglected for thirty days after such presentment to pay the same. Before any execution shall be issued on any judgment recovered upon such a claim, a notice of the recovery thereof shall also be given to the comptroller, and he shall be allowed ten days to provide for its payment by the issue of revenue bonds in the usual manner according to law.

Quorum of board.

Actions on claims.

Notice to comptroller of judgments.

SEC. 106. The mayor shall, from time to time, appoint

Commissioners of accounts.

and remove at pleasure two persons, who, together with the president of the department of taxes and assessments, shall be commissioners of accounts. It shall be their duty, once in three months, and oftener if they deem it proper, to examine all vouchers and accounts in the offices of the comptroller and chamberlain, and to make and publish, in the City Record, a detailed statement of the financial condition of the city, showing the amount of its funded and floating debt, the amount received and expended since the last preceding report, with a classification of the sources of revenue and expenditure, and such other information as they shall deem proper. They shall from time to time make an examination of the expenses of the several departments and officers, and make such recommendations to the board of apportionment, and other officers, with reference thereto, and particularly with reference to salaries and duties, as they deem advisable. Any one of such commissioners shall have authority at any time to make any such examination, and such two appointed commissioners shall be paid a reasonable compensation, to be fixed as other expenditures by the board of apportionment, not exceeding three thousand dollars each annually.

Duties of.

Salary.

Departments to furnish certified copies of all papers required.

SEC. 107. The heads of all departments, except the police department, and the chiefs of each and every bureau of said departments, or any of them, except the police department, shall, with reasonable promptness, furnish to any taxpayer desiring the same a true and certified copy of any book, account or paper kept by such department, bureau, or officer, or such part thereof as may be demanded, upon payment in advance of five cents for every hundred words thereof by the person demanding the same. All books, accounts and papers, in any department or bureau thereof, except the police department, shall at all times be open to the inspection of any taxpayer, subject to any reasonable rules and regulations in regard to the time and manner of such inspection as such department, bureau or officer may make in regard to the same, in order to secure the safety of such books, accounts and papers, and the proper use of them by the department, bureau or officer. In case such inspection shall be refused, such taxpayer, on his sworn petition, describing the particular book, account or paper that he desires to inspect, may, upon notice of not less than one day to such department, bureau or officer, apply to any justice of the supreme court for an order that he be allowed to make such inspection as such justice shall by his order authorize, and such order shall specify the time and manner of such inspection.

Books open to the public.

Order of court in case of refusal to inspect books.

SEC. 108. It shall be the duty of the comptroller to publish in the City Record, two months before the election of charter officers, a full and detailed statement of the receipts and expenditures of the corporation during the year ending on the first day of the month in which such publication is made, and the cash balance or surplus; and in every such statement the different sources of city

Financial statement to be published in City Record.

revenue, and the amount received from each, the several appropriations made, the objects for which the same were made, and the amount of moneys expended under each, the moneys borrowed on the credit of the corporation, the authority under which each loan was made, and the terms on which the same was obtained, shall be clearly and particularly specified.

Summary examination of all officers.

SEC. 109. Any alderman, commissioner, head of department, chief of bureau, deputy thereof, or clerk therein, or other officer of the corporation or person, may, if a judge shall so order, be summarily examined upon an order to be made on application based on an affidavit of the mayor or of the comptroller, or any five aldermen, or any commissioners of accounts, or of any five citizens who are taxpayers, requiring such examination, and signed by any justice of the supreme court of the first judicial department, directing such examination to be publicly made at the chambers of said court, or at tbe office of said department, on a day and hour to be named, not less, however, than forty-eight hours after personal service of said order. Such examination shall be confined to an inquiry into any alleged wrongful diversion or misapplication of any moneys or fund, or any violation of the provisions of law, or any want of mechanical qualification for any inspectorship of public work, or any neglect of duty in acting as such inspector, or any delinquency charged in said affidavit touching the office or the discharge or neglect of duty, of which it is alleged in the

Subject of inquiry.

application for said order that such alderman, head of department, or other aforementioned officer or persons, has knowledge or information. Such alderman, commissioner, head of department, clerk, or other aforesaid officer or person shall answer such pertinent questions relative thereto, and produce such books and papers in his custody, or under his control, as the justice shall direct, and the examination may be continued from time to time, as such justice may order, but the answer of the party charged shall not be used against him in any criminal proceeding; provided, however, that for all false answers on material points he shall be subject to the pains and penalties of the crime of perjury. The proceedings may be continued before any other justice in said district, and other witnesses, as well as the parties making such application, may, in the discretion of said justice, be compelled to attend and be examined touching such alleged delinquencies. Such justice may punish any refusal to attend such examination or to answer any questions pursuant to his order, as for a contempt of court, and shall have as full power and authority to enforce obedience to the order or directions of himself, or any other justice, as any justice of the supreme court may now have, or shall possess, to enforce obedience or to punish contempt in any case or matter whatever, and shall impose costs upon those promoting such an examination not exceeding two hundred and fifty dollars, if he thinks there was no probable cause for making the application hereinbefore provided for, the said costs to be paid

Books and papers may be produced in court.

Witnesses may be examined.

Powers of justice.

Costs, how imposed.

to the officer or person examined, and for which the said officer or person may have judgment and an execution. The examination hereinbefore provided for shall be reduced to writing, and be filed in the office of the county clerk of the county of New York, and be at all reasonable times accessible to the public, and notice of the same given to the department in which said officer is employed.

Examination to be filed.

Weekly abstract of business of departments to be published.

SEC. 110. In every department or board there shall be kept a record of all its transactions, which shall be accessible to the public, and once a week a brief abstract, omitting formal language, shall be made of all transactions, and of all contracts awarded and entered into for work and material of every description, which abstract shall contain the name or names, and residences by street and number, of the party or parties to the contract, and of their sureties, if any. A copy of such abstract shall be promptly transmitted to the person designated to prepare the City Record, and shall be published therein. Notice of all appointments and removals from office, and all changes of salaries, shall, in like manner, within one week after they are made, be transmitted to and published in the City Record.

Appointments and removals to be published.

City Record.

SEC. 111. There shall be published daily (Sundays and legal holidays excepted), under a contract to be made as hereinafter provided, a paper to be known as the "City Record." The mayor, corporation counsel and commissioner of public works shall appoint a proper person, together with such assistants as may be required to supervise the preparation and publication of the same, and they shall also fix the rates of compensation of said supervisor and his assistants. All the expenses connected with its publication and distribution, except the salary of the person appointed to supervise the same, and the salaries of his assistants, shall be covered by a contract for printing, to be made in the same manner as other contracts. The board of estimate and apportionment shall provide for all the necessary expenses of establishing and conducting the said City Record. There shall be inserted in said City Record nothing aside from such official matters as are in this act expressly authorized. The contract for the publication of the City Record shall provide for furnishing, free of charge, to the city not more than one thousand copies thereof, also for a gratuitous distribution to every newspaper regularly printed in the city of New York, when it shall apply for the same, of two copies, and to every public library or public institution in said city which shall apply for the same, of one copy. Copies of the same shall be sold by the publisher at a price to be fixed by the officers making the contract, and the proceeds thereof shall be paid over to the city. All advertising required to be done for the city, and all notices required by law or ordinance to be published in corporation papers, shall be inserted, at the public expense, only in the City Record, and a publication therein shall be a sufficient compliance with any law or ordinance requiring publication of such matters or notices; but there may be

Expenses of publishing.

Contract.

Sale of City Record.

Advertising

Advertisements in other papers.

inserted in two morning and two evening and two weekly papers published in the English language, and in one newspaper published in the German language, all in said city, to be designated by the mayor, corporation counsel and commissioner of public works, annually, brief advertisements calling attention to any contracts intended to be awarded, or bonds to be sold, and referring for full information to said City Record. No money shall be paid from the city treasury for advertising hereafter done except such as is herein authorized, and no action shall be maintained or judgment obtained against the city for any advertising hereafter done except such as is herein authorized. The copies of the City Record furnished to the city shall be distributed to the several departments and officers, and to such persons and in such manner as the mayor shall direct. All printing for said city, including the printing of the City Record, shall be executed, and all stationery shall be supplied, under contracts, to be entered into by the mayor, corporation counsel and commissioner of public works. The first contract for printing the City Record shall be awarded after an advertisement in the five daily newspapers printed in said city having the largest circulation therein, for at least two weeks, inviting proposals. All proposals for printing and stationery shall be based upon specifications to be filed in the department of public works, which shall set forth with accuracy the number of every description of printed blanks; also each description of stationery or blank books in ordinary use in the board of aldermen and the respective departments

Contract for printing City Record.

Stationery and blanks.

and likely to be required during the year for which such contract is to be given; and the bids shall be given for such number of each printed description of blanks, or of each article of stationery (including under the head of stationery, letter or writing paper, or envelopes, with printed headings or indorsements) as are specified, and for such additional number as may be required, giving the price for blanks of every description, and the price of all other printing "per thousand ems," or for "rule and figure work;" separate contracts shall be made with the lowest bidder for any one description of printing, or any article of stationery involving an expense of more than five hundred dollars. Ten per cent. of the amount becoming due, from time to time, shall be withheld by the comptroller until the completion of the contract; and in case the contractor shall fail to fulfill the same to the satisfaction of the mayor, corporation counsel and commissioner of public works, then they may declare said contract to be annulled, and they shall immediately give notice for other bids for such printing during the remainder of the term of contract. No judgment shall be recovered against the city for printing or stationery done or furnished after the passage of this act, unless done or furnished under a contract where, under the provisions of this act, a contract is necessary, or under a valid contract or a contract now in force, or unless upon evidence of a contract made as provided in this section. Separate contracts may be made at any time for engraving, lithographing, woodcuts, maps or other picture work, as the same may be required; but

Ten per cent. on contract to be withheld.

Separate contracts for engravings, maps, etc.

nothing herein contained shall be construed to require a separate contract for each engraving, lithograph or wood-cut or map, unless the officers aforesaid shall deem the same advisable for the interest of the city. No more than one thousand copies of any message of the mayor, or report of any head of a department, and no more than five hundred copies of any report of a committee of the board of aldermen, or board of assistant aldermen, shall be printed apart from the City Record. Neither the work known as the Manual of the Common Council nor any similar work shall be printed at the public expense; but there shall be published in the City Record, within the month of January in each year, a list of all subordinates employed in any department (except laborers), with their salaries, and residences by street numbers, and all changes in such subordinates or salaries shall be so published within one week after they are made. It shall be the duty of all heads of departments to furnish, to the person appointed to supervise the publication of the City Record, everything required to be inserted therein. The said person shall have the power to make requisitions in writing upon the heads of departments to furnish the information necessary to make up such list according to rules prescribed by him and approved by the comptroller; and such information must be supplied by the department within ten days after such requisition. He shall have power to require such information in the same manner, every three months, and all other information in the control of said heads of departments, necessary to perform

Copies of messages and reports limited.

City Manual.

List of all officers and subordinates to be published yearly.

Powers of supervisor of City Record.

his duties under this section. He shall include in his list the number of laborers, designating the department in which they are employed, and, if practicable, the numbers employed in the prosecution of specific work, and the amounts paid to them. He shall also cause to be printed in each issue of said City Record a separate statement of the hours during which all public offices in the city are open for business, and at which each court regularly opens and adjourns, as well as of the places where such offices are kept and such courts are held. The detailed canvass of votes at every election shall be published at the expense of the city only in the City Record. The mayor may order the insertion of any official matter or report in the City Record.

Official hours for business of all departments to be published daily.

Election canvass.

[*Amended by adding the following—sec.* 1, *chap.* 631, *laws of* 1875.] Nothing herein contained shall apply to any printing or supplies of stationery for the mayor, aldermen, and commonalty of the city of New York, where, by the concurrent vote of the mayor, counsel to the corporation, and the commissioner of public works, it shall be decided to have such printing done or such stationery furnished without contract let after advertisements for bids or proposals; but in such cases such printing shall be done and such stationery procured in the manner, and on such terms and conditions as the said officers shall deem to be for the best interests of the city.*

When printing and supplies may be furnished without contract.

* See Appendix, K.

SEC. 112. [*As amended by sec.* 20, *chap.* 757, *laws of* 1873.] The mayor, comptroller, president of the board of aldermen, and the president of the department of taxes and assessments, shall constitute a board of estimate and apportionment, who shall, annually, between the first day of August and the first day of November, meet, and, by the affirmative vote of all the members, make a provisional estimate of the amounts required to pay the expenses of conducting the public business of the city and county of New York, in each department and branch thereof, and the board of education for the then next ensuing financial year. In such provisional estimate they shall include such sum as may be necessary for the payment of the interest on the bonds of the said city and county, which shall become due and payable within said year, and such sum as shall be necessary to pay the principal of any bonds and stocks which may become due and payable from taxes during said year, and also so much as may be necessary to pay the proportion of the state tax required to be paid by the city and county of New York in said year. Such provisional estimate shall be prepared in such detail as to the aggregate sum allowed to each department and bureau as the said board of apportionment shall deem advisable. For the purpose of making said provisional estimate, the heads of departments and the board of education shall, at least thirty days before the said provisional estimate is required to be

Board of estimate and apportionment.

Provisional estimate.

Provisional estimate, what to contain.

Estimates in detail.

Heads of departments to furnish statement.

made as herein provided, send to the board of apportionment an estimate in writing, herein called a departmental estimate, of the amount of expenditure, specifying in detail the objects thereof, required in their respective departments, including a statement of each of the salaries of their officers, clerks, employees and subordinates. The same statement as to salaries and expenditure shall be made by all other officers, persons and boards having power to fix or authorize them. A duplicate of these departmental estimates and statements shall be made at the same time to the board of aldermen. The board of apportionment shall consider such departmental estimates and other statements in making the provisional estimates herein provided, and in approving the salaries of the officers, clerks and other persons before named. After such provisional estimate is made by the board of apportionment, it shall be submitted by said board, with their reasons for it in detail, within ten days, to the board of aldermen, whereupon a special meeting of said board shall be called to consider such estimate, and the same shall simultaneously be published in the City Record; and it shall be their duty carefully to consider and investigate the said provisional estimate and the reasons assigned therefor; but such consideration and investigation shall not continue beyond fifteen days. Any objections to or rectifications of said provisional estimate made by said board of aldermen shall be

Duplicate estimate submitted to board of aldermen.

Corrections may be made.

made by said board in writing, and transmitted by the clerk thereof to the board of apportionment, who shall proceed to the consideration of such objections or rectifications, and after such consideration shall make a final estimate. Should the said board overrule the objections or suggestions made by the board of aldermen, the reasons for such action shall be published in the City Record. After the final estimate is made, in accordance herewith, it shall be signed by the members, and when so signed the said several sums shall be and become appropriated to the several purposes and departments therein named. The said estimate shall be filed in the office of the comptroller and published in the City Record. The aggregate amount so estimated shall be certified by the comptroller to the supervisors of the county of New York; and it shall be the duty of said supervisors, and they are hereby empowered and directed annually to cause to be raised, according to law, and collected by tax upon the estates, real and personal, subject to taxation within the city and county of New York, the said amounts so estimated and certified as aforesaid. The first meeting of said board in every year shall be called by notice from the mayor, personally served upon the members of said board. Subsequent meetings shall be called as the said board shall direct. At such meetings the mayor shall preside, and one of the number shall act as secretary In addition to the estimate herein provided for, the

Final estimate to be signed and filed.

Supervisors to meet and consider such estimate, and raise the same by tax.

Meetings of supervisors.

said board may, at any time, as occasion may require, by the affirmative vote of three members, authorize the issue of any stocks or bonds for the purpose of withdrawing or taking up at maturity any stocks or bonds for the purpose outstanding; but the said bonds or their proceeds shall be applied exclusively to the payment, purchase and extinction of such maturing bonds in such manner that the aggregate of the stocks or bonds of said city outstanding shall not be increased thereby for a longer period than is necessary in effecting said change. The said board of apportionment may, from time to time, by the affirmative vote of three members, authorize the issue of the whole or any portion of any stock or bonds which are now by law authorized to be issued, upon compliance with the provisions of law authorizing them. The said board of apportionment may, from time to time, on the application of the head of any department, authorize the transfer, from one bureau or purpose to another in the same department, of any sum theretofore appropriated for the purpose of such department or bureau, but no department or officer shall incur any expense in excess of sum appropriated. The board of apportionment may, within forty days after the passage hereof, revise and readjust, in accordance with the provisions hereof, the apportionment heretofore made. All the provisions of law creating any board of apportionment and audit, or either, and providing

May authorize issue of stocks or bonds.

Appropriations, how transferred.

Repeal of certain provisions.

for and requiring an audit and allowance of claims by said board, are hereby repealed; but such repeal shall not, prior to the organization of the board of apportionment by this act created, affect any act heretofore done or directed to be done; but all the powers now possessed by any such board, not inconsistent with the provisions of this act, are hereby continued and vested in the board hereby created and authorized, and all actions or proceedings in which the mayor, aldermen and commonalty of the city of New York are plaintiffs or defendants, shall have a preference, and may be moved out of their order on the calendar. Any balances of appropriations remaining unexpended, after allowing sufficient to satisfy all claims payable therefrom, may at any time, after the expiration of the year for which they were made, be transferred by the comptroller, with the approval of said board of estimate and apportionment, to the general fund of the city, and applied to the reduction of taxation.

Unexpended balances.

[*As amended by sec.* 2, *chap.* 308, *laws of* 1874.] The said board of estimate and apportionment shall have the power at any time to transfer any appropriation for any year which may be found, by the head of the department for which such appropriation shall have been made, to be in excess of the amount required or deemed to be necessary for the purposes or objects thereof, to such other purposes or objects for

Unexpended appropriations may be transferred.

which the appropriations are insufficient, or such as may require the same; and if it is found at the time when the estimate is made of the expenses of conducting the public business of the city of New York for the next succeeding fiscal year, that there will be a surplus or balance remaining unexpended of any appropriation then existing at the end of the current fiscal year, such surplus may be applied to like purposes in the next succeeding year.*

Contesting elections, costs of, how paid.

SEC. 113. No appropriation or payment for the contesting of the office of mayor, or any seat in the board of aldermen, or office in any department, or the office of any officer whose salary is paid from the city treasury, shall be made to any but the prevailing party. Nor shall any such appropriation or payment be made to such prevailing party, except upon the written certificates of the chief officer of the law department and of the chief justice of the court of common pleas of the city and county of New York, as to the value of the services rendered in the case. In case an officer or clerk is ordered to be examined, in pursuance of the provisions hereinbefore contained, the law department shall assign some one from his department as counsel to the officer or clerk making the application, but should such officer or clerk see fit to employ other counsel than that assigned by the law department, then, and in that event, no appropriation or payment shall be made for his or their

Counsel in case of examination of officer or clerk.

See Appendix, L, M, and N.

payment except upon a certificate of the justice or justices before whom the proceedings have been had that there was probable cause for taking such proceedings.

City officers not to hold state or federal office;

SEC. 114. Any person holding office, whether by election or appointment, who shall, during his term of office, accept, hold, or retain any other civil office of honor, trust, or emolument under the government of the United States (except commissioners for the taking of bail, or register of any court), or of the State (except the office of notary public or commissioner of deeds, or office of the national guard), or who shall hold or accept any other office connected with the government of the city of New York, or who shall accept a seat in the legislature, shall be deemed thereby to have vacated every office held by him under the city government. No person shall hold two city or county offices, except as expressly provided in this act; nor shall any officer under the city government hold or retain an office under the county government, except when he holds such office ex-officio, by virtue of an act of the legislature; and in such case he shall draw no salary for such ex-officio office.

nor more than city or county office.

Consulting engineers.

[*Amended by adding the following—sec.* 21, *chap.* 757, *laws of* 1873.] This section shall not be construed to apply to civil or consulting engineers who may be appointed to superintend any specific work, on the part of the city of New York.

SEC. 115. [*As amended by sec.* 1, *chap.* 476, *laws*

of 1875.] Whenever the commissioner of public works of the city of New York shall certify and report to the board of aldermen of said city that the safety, health, or convenience of the public requires the repavement of any streets, avenues, or public places in said city, said board of aldermen shall have the power to direct by ordinance or resolution, the repavement of said streets, avenues, or public places, in the manner specified and of the materials approved of and recommended by said commissioner of public works, which work shall be done by and under the direction of the department of public works, according to law. In case any of the streets, avenues, or public places in said city shall have been once paved, and the expense thereof assessed upon the owners of adjoining and benefited property, the cost of the repaving thereof shall be borne by a general assessment upon all taxable property in said city. The cost of repaving the streets, avenues, or public places, in accordance with the provisions of this act, shall be included in the estimate of the department of public works, shall be appropriated by the board of estimate and apportionment, certified by the comptroller according to law, and inserted and included in the annual tax levies, and raised and collected by tax upon the estates subject to taxation in the city and county of New York, provided that the amount so appropriated and raised shall not exceed the sum of five hundred thousand dollars in any one single year.*

Petition for repaving, etc., streets.

Only one assessment.

Repaving streets.

* See Appendix, G.

Annual salaries of chief officers.

SEC 116. The annual salaries to be paid to persons herein named shall be as follows, and such salaries shall be in full for all services rendered by them to the city or county, in any capacity whatever:

To the mayor, twelve thousand dollars.

To the comptroller, ten thousand dollars.

To the commissioner of public works, ten thousand dollars.

To the corporation counsel, fifteen thousand dollars; and all legal costs collected by him shall be paid into the treasury of the city.

To the president of the board of police, eight thousand dollars.

To the commissioners of police, other than the president, six thousand dollars each.

To the president of the department of parks, six thousand five hundred dollars.

To the commissioners of parks, other than the president, nothing.

To the president of the fire department, seven thousand five hundred dollars.

To the fire commissioners, other than the president, five thousand dollars each.

To the president of the department of charities and correction, six thousand five hundred dollars.

To the commissioners of charities and correction, other than the president, five thousand dollars each.

To the president of the health department, six thousand five hundred dollars.

To the commissioner of health, other than the president, five thousand dollars.

[*Amended by sec.* 23, *chap.* 757, *laws of* 1873.] To the members of the board of aldermen, other than the president, four thousand dollars each, and to the members of the board of assistant aldermen, four thousand dollars each during their present term of office.

To the president of the board of aldermen, five thousand dollars.

To the president of the department of taxes and assessments, six thousand five hundred dollars.

To the commissioners of taxes and assessments, other than the president, five thousand dollars each.

To the president of the department of docks, six thousand five hundred dollars.

To the commissioners of docks, other than the president, three thousand dollars each.

[*Amended by sec.* 10, *chap.* 547, *laws of* 1874.] To the superintendent of buildings, six thousand five hundred dollars.

[*Amended by sec.* 23, *chap.* 757, *laws of* 1873.] To the commissioners of accounts, appointed by the mayor, three thousand dollars each.

Salary of subordinates.

No subordinate in any department shall receive a greater salary than the highest salary paid to the head of the department, except the superintendent of police, whose salary shall not exceed ten thousand dollars per annum. The salaries of the justices of the district courts is hereby fixed at eight thousand dollars each per annum.

Salary of justices.

Expiration of terms of office.

SEC. 117. The terms of office of the present commissioners of police, except as hereinbefore expressly provided, fire commissioners, commissioners of charities and correction, commissioners of docks, commissioners of health, commissioners of parks, except as hereinbefore expressly provided, commissioners of taxes and assessments, superintendent of buildings, commissioner of jurors, city marshals, inspectors of weights and measures, members of all commissions or boards appointed to superintend the construction or repair of any public building in the city of New York, and of all commissions and boards heretofore appointed by the mayor,. or the mayor and aldermen, save and except as hereinbefore expressly provided, and all members of any board, and all persons whatever heretofore appointed by the comptroller; of the chamberlain and all other officers hereinbefore authorized to be appointed by the mayor and board of aldermen, shall cease, terminate and expire on the first day of May, one thousand eight hundred and seventy-three, unless an appointment of a successor shall be sooner made as hereinbefore provided, in which case the term of office of the present incumbent shall cease, and the person so appointed shall enter upon his office on the first Monday succeeding such appointment; and no appointment of any subordinate in any department, made after the passage of this act and before said date, shall be valid beyond such date. The terms of office of the superintendent of police, the surgeons of police, the chief engineer of the fire department, the inspector of the fire apparatus, the superintendent of horses, and the superintendent of the repair yard in the fire department, the fire marshal and his deputies, shall cease and determine five days after the appointment of the head of the police and fire department respectively, and the terms of all subordinates in every department, except officers and men of the police force and the firemen and officers of the fire companies, shall cease and determine as soon as the heads of the department herein provided to be appointed shall appoint others in their places. Upon the appointment of their successors all the foregoing officers shall deliver over to such successors all property of every kind, and all books and papers in their use and possession, respectively, belonging to the city or any department thereof. The provisions of this section, relating to the vacating of any of the offices therein mentioned and the delivery of property, may be enforced by mandamus. But nothing in this section shall affect exceptions and savings in the twenty-fifth section of this act contained.

Property transferred to successors.

SEC. 118. The several departments shall continue to

General powers.

possess the same powers and perform the same duties as heretofore, except as herein otherwise provided.

City exempt from certain acts.

SEC. 119. The city of New York is hereby excepted from the provisions of an act entitled an act to establish a metropolitan police district, and to provide for the government thereof, passed April fifteen, eighteen hundred and fifty-seven, and of the acts amendatory thereof, and any sections of statutes and provisions of law which created said district are hereby repealed; and the city of New York is also hereby excepted from the provisions of the act entitled an act to create a metropolitan sanitary district and board of health therein, for the preservation of life and health, and to prevent spread of disease, passed February twenty-sixth, eighteen hundred and sixty-six, and of the acts amendatory thereof, and any sections of statutes and provisions of law which created said district are hereby repealed; and the city of New York is also hereby excepted from the provisions of an act entitled an act to create a metropolitan fire district, and establish a fire department therein, passed March thirtieth, eighteen hundred and sixty-five, and the acts amendatory thereof, and any sections of statutes and provisions of law which created said district are hereby repealed. The act to amend the charter of the city of New York, passed April seventh, eighteen hundred and thirty; and the act to amend the charter of the city of New York, passed April second, eighteen hundred and forty-nine; and the act to amend an act entitled an act to amend the charter

Acts repealed.

of the city of New York, passed April second, eighteen hundred and forty-nine, passed July eleventh, eighteen hundred and fifty-one; and the act further to amend the charter of the city of New York, passed April twelfth, eighteen hundred and fifty-three; and the act supplementary to an act entitled an act further to amend the charter of the city of New York, passed April twelfth, eighteen hundred and fifty-three, passed June fourteenth, eighteen hundred and fifty-three; and the act to amend the charter of the city of New York, passed April fourteen, eighteen hundred and fifty-seven; and the act relative to the charter of the city of New York, passed April three, eighteen hundred and sixty-three; and the act to make provision for the government of the city of New York, passed June third, eighteen hundred and sixty-eight; and the act entitled an act to reorganize the local government of the city of New York, passed April fifth, eighteen hundred and seventy; and the act entitled an act to make further provisions for the government of the city of New York, passed April twenty-six, eighteen hundred and seventy (save sections twenty-seven and twenty-nine thereof); and the sixth section of an act entitled an act concerning the police life insurance fund, and the powers and duties of the police department of the city of New York, passed March seventeen, eighteen hundred and seventy-one; and the act entitled an act to amend an act to reorganize the local government of the city of New York, passed April fifth, eighteen hundred and seventy, passed April the eighteenth, eighteen

Police life insurance fund.

Exception to repeal.

hundred and seventy-one (save so much of section five thereof as relates to the establishment of a scale of water rents, and sections six and seven of said act); and the act entitled an act to make provision for the local governments of the city and county of New York, passed April nineteen, eighteen hundred and seventy-one, so far as said act relates to the city of New York, are hereby repealed; and all acts or parts of acts inconsistent with the provisions of this act are also hereby repealed; but the repeal of the act hereinabove cited of April fifth, eighteen hundred and seventy, and the acts passed subsequently thereto and hereinabove cited or referred to, so far as the same or either of them relate to any department by this act created, shall not take effect until the organization of any such department as provided for in this act. The charters of the city of New York, known as Dongan and Montgomerie charters, so far as the same or either of them are now in force, not inconsistent with the provisions of this act, shall continue and remain in full force. This section shall not prejudice or affect any right accrued or legal proceeding commenced by reason of anything contained in the acts hereby repealed, and so accrued and commenced before this act takes effect, except so far as herein specially provided for. The ordinances of the common council of the city of New York, in force on the first day of April, eighteen hundred and seventy, and all ordinances passed and adopted since the first day of May, eighteen hundred and seventy, and in force at the time of the passage of this act, are hereby revived and continued

Dongan and Montgomerie charters.

Ordinances continued in force.

in full force as city ordinances, subject to modification, amendment or repeal by the common council of said city.*

Terms of office mentioned in section 17 limited.

SEC. 120. [*As amended by sec.* 24, *chap.* 757, *laws of* 1873.] This act shall take effect immediately, except as otherwise provided in the previous section; but nothing therein contained shall be in any wise held to extend or continue the term of office of any of the persons mentioned in section one hundred and seventeen, beyond the first day of May, eighteen hundred and seventy-three.

* See Appendix, O.

APPENDIX.

(A.)

Chapter 515.

An Act to amend an act entitled "An act to reorganize the local government of the city of New York," passed April thirtieth, eighteen hundred and seventy-three.

Passed May 21, 1874; three-fifths being present.

The People of the State of New York, represented in Senate and Assembly, do enact as follows:

Section 1. Section four of chapter three hundred and thirty-five of the laws of eighteen hundred and seventy-three, entitled "An act to reorganize the local government of the city of New York," is hereby amended so as to read as follows:

§ 4. The board of aldermen now in office shall hold office until the first Monday in January, in the year eighteen hundred and seventy-five, the same being the term for which they were elected. There shall be twenty-two aldermen elected at the general state election which shall occur in the year eighteen hundred and seventy-four, three of whom shall be elected in each senate district, except the eighth senate district, and shall be residents of the district in which they are elected, but no voter shall vote for more than two of said aldermen. In the territory comprised within the eighth senate district, and the twenty-third and twenty-fourth wards, there shall be elected four aldermen, and the aldermen to be elected in said district may reside either in said eighth senate district or in the twenty-third and twenty-fourth wards, but no voter shall vote for more than three of the said

Aldermen, term of office.

When elected.

Aldermen at large.

aldermen. There shall also be elected six aldermen at large to be voted for on a separate ballot, but no voter shall vote for more than four of the said aldermen at large, and the voters of the twenty-third and twenty-fourth wards of said city are hereby authorized and empowered to vote for aldermen at large. The members of the board of aldermen shall hold office for the space of one year, and shall take office on the first Monday in January, next succeeding their election, at noon. Annually thereafter, at the general state election, there shall be elected a full board of aldermen as hereinbefore provided. Any

Vacancy, election to fill.

vacancy now existing, or which may hereafter occur, in *either* the board of aldermen* by reason of the death or resignation, or of any other cause, of a member of either of said boards, shall be filled by election by the board in which such vacancy exists or shall arise, by a vote of a majority of all the members elected to said board; and the person so elected to fill any such vacancy shall serve until the first day of January, at noon, next succeeding the first general election occurring not less than thirty days after the happening of such vacancy, but not beyond the expiration of the term in which the vacancy shall occur; and at such election a person shall be elected to serve the remainder, if any, of such unexpired term. From and after the termination of the term of office of the board of assistant aldermen as herein provided, the board of aldermen shall alone constitute the common council and shall exercise the entire legislative powers of the said city.

SEC. 4.* This act shall take effect immediately.

* So in the original.

(**B.**)

Chapter 304.

An Act to consolidate the government of the city and county of New York, and further to regulate the same.

Passed April 30, 1874; three-fifths being present.

The People of the State of New York, represented in Senate and Assembly, do enact as follows:

Section 1. The county of New York and the corporation known by the name of "the mayor, aldermen, and commonalty of the city of New York" shall be one body corporate and politic by the said name; and all the rights, property, interests, claims, and demands of the county of New York, and of the supervisors or board of supervisors of the said county of New York, are hereby vested in and shall henceforth belong to the said corporation; but nothing contained in this act shall abrogate or impair or in anywise affect any existing right or interest, except to vest it in the said corporation.

Consolidation.

Existing rights unimpaired.

Sec. 2. For all purposes the local administration and government of the city and county of New York shall be in and be performed by the one corporation aforesaid. All charges and liabilities now existing against said county, or which may hereafter arise or accrue in said city and county of New York, and which, but for this act, would be charges against or liabilities of said county, shall be henceforth deemed and taken to be charges against or liabilities of said corporation, and shall be defrayed or answered unto by it. All bonds, stocks, contracts and obligations of the said county and of the said board of supervisors, now existing, shall henceforth be deemed such of and against said corporation, and all such that are or may be authorized or required to be hereafter issued or entered into, shall be issued or entered into by and in the name of the said corporation.

County charges and liabilities merged in the city corporation.

Powers and duties of board of supervisors transferred to board of aldermen.

SEC. 3. All the powers and duties that now are or hereafter may be conferred or charged upon the board of supervisors of the said city and county shall be exercised and performed by the board of aldermen of said city as such, subject, nevertheless, to the like power of approval or rejection by the mayor of said city, as is or may be required by law in respect to acts of the common council of said city, except that when by the constitution or laws of this state any action is specifically required to be taken by the board of supervisors of said city and county, which cannot, under any power conferred by this act or otherwise, be taken in any other manner, such action may be taken by the said board of aldermen as the board of supervisors of the said city and county.

Funds held by county treasurer.

SEC. 4. All funds and moneys now held by or payable to any officer as county treasurer of the said city and county shall henceforth be deemed to be held by him solely as the funds and moneys of said corporation, except such funds and moneys as shall be held by and payable into the treasury of the state of New York.

SEC. 5. This act shall take effect immediately.

(C.)

Chapter 305.

AN ACT explanatory of "An act to consolidate the government of the city and county of New York, and further to regulate the same."

Passed April 30, 1874; three-fifths being present.

The People of the State of New York, represented in Senate and Assembly, do enact as follows:

SECTION 1. Nothing in the act entitled "An act to consolidate the government of the city and county of New York, and further to regulate the same," shall be construed to affect the election and appointment of county officers whose election or appointment is provided for by the constitution of this state, the apportionment of members of assembly, or any other purposes for which the city and county of New York is recognized in the constitution as one of the counties of this state. County officers.

SEC. 2. This act shall take effect immediately.

(D.)

Chapter 757.

AN ACT to amend chapter three hundred and thirty-five of the laws of eighteen hundred and seventy-three, entitled "An act to reorganize the local government of the city of New York," passed April thirteenth,* eighteen hundred and seventy-three.

Passed June 13, 1873; three-fifths being present.

The People of the State of New York, represented in Senate and Assembly, do enact as follows:

SECTION 1. Section four of chapter three hundred and thirty-five of the laws of eighteen hundred and seventy-three, entitled "An act to reorganize the local government of the city of New York," passed April thirtieth, eighteen hundred and seventy-three, is hereby amended (see chap. 515, Laws 1874).

SEC. 2. Section seven of said chapter is hereby amended so as to read as follows:

§ 7. Every member expelled from either board shall thereby forfeit all his rights and powers as alderman or assistant alderman. Expulsion.

* So in original.

SEC. 3. Section eight of said chapter is hereby amended so as to read as follows :

Meetings.

§ 8. The stated and occasional meetings of each board shall be regulated by its own resolutions and rules, and both boards may meet at the same time or on different days, as they may severally deem expedient.

SEC. 4. Section ten of said chapter is hereby amended so as to read as follows :

§ 10. The mayor shall return such ordinance or resolution to the board in which it originated within ten days after receiving it, or at the next meeting of such board after the expiration of said ten days.

Clerk of board of aldermen, his duties.

SEC. 5. The first period or sentence of section fifteen is hereby amended so as to read as follows : "The clerk of the board of aldermen shall, by virtue of his office, be clerk of the common council and of the board of supervisors, and shall perform all the duties heretofore performed by the clerk of the common council, except such as shall be assigned to the clerk of the board of assistant aldermen, without additional compensation to that paid him as clerk of the board of aldermen."

SEC. 6. The tenth subdivision of the seventeenth section of said chapter is hereby amended, by adding thereto, at the end thereof, the words following: "and to provide for regulating, grading, flagging, curbing, guttering and lighting streets, roads, places and avenues."

SEC. 7. Section twenty is hereby amended so as to read as follows:

Mayor to continue in office.

§ 20. The mayor in office on April twenty-ninth, eighteen hundred and seventy-three, shall hold office until the first day of January, in the year eighteen hundred and seventy-five. The mayor shall be the chief executive officer of the corporation ; shall be elected at a general election, and hold his office for the term of two years, commencing on the first day of January next after his election. The first election for mayor under this act shall be at the general election in November, in the year eighteen hundred and seventy-four.

SEC. 8. The twenty-ninth section of the said chapter is hereby amended by adding at the end of the seventh clause or sentence of said section the words: "But this provision shall not apply to work done or supplies furnished, not involving the expenditure of more than one thousand dollars, pursuant to section ninety-one of this act." And the said section is further amended by adding at the end thereof the words following: "The comptroller shall furnish to each head of department, weekly, a statement of the unexpended balance of the appropriation of his department; wages and salaries, including payments for the board of education, may be paid upon pay-rolls, upon which each person named thereon shall separately receipt for the amount paid to such person, and in every case of payment upon a pay-roll, the warrant for the aggregate amount of wages and salaries included therein may be made payable to the superintendent, principal teacher, foreman or other officer designated for the purpose."

Comptroller to furnish weekly statement.

Wages and salaries may be paid upon pay-rolls.

SEC. 9. Section seventy-three of the said chapter is hereby amended by striking out of the same the words "ninety-seven" and inserting in place thereof the words "ninety-one."

SEC. 10. Section seventy-five of said chapter is hereby amended so as to read as follows:

§ 75. No money belonging to the city, or city and county, of New York, raised by taxation upon the property of the citizens thereof, shall be appropriated in aid of any religious or denominational school, neither shall any property, real or personal, belonging to said city, or said city and county, be disposed of to any such school, except upon the sale thereof at public auction after the same has been duly advertised, at which sale such school shall be the highest bidder, and upon payment of the sum so bid into the city treasury; neither shall any property belonging to the city, or city and county, be leased to any school under the control of any religious or denominational institution, except upon such terms as city property may be leased to private parties after the same has been duly advertised.

Money not to be appropriated to religious or denominational schools.

SEC. 11. Section seventy-eight of said chapter is hereby amended so as to read as follows:

Fire department, qualifications for membership.

§ 78. No person shall ever be appointed to membership in the fire department, or continue to hold membership therein, who is not a citizen of the United States, or who has ever been convicted of crime, or who cannot read and write understandingly in the English language, or who shall not have resided within the state one year.

Board of health, powers.

SEC. 12. Section eighty-second of said chapter is hereby amended by adding thereto as follows: "The authority, duty, and powers conferred or enjoined upon the metropolitan board of health by chapter seventy-four of the laws of eighteen hundred and sixty-six, and the several acts amendatory thereof, and by any other subsequent laws of this state, and upon the several officers and members of said board, not inconsistent with the provisions of this act, are hereby conferred upon and vested in or enjoined upon, and shall hereafter be exclusively exercised in the city of New York, by the health department and board of health, created by this act, and by the officers of the said board of health and the said health department, and the same are to be exercised in the manner specified in the said chapter seventy-four of the laws of eighteen hundred and sixty-six, and the several acts amendatory thereof, and by any other subsequent laws of the state, and in conformity to the provisions of this act."

SEC. 13. The eighty-third section of said chapter is hereby amended by striking out therefrom the words "for the construction."

SEC. 14. The eighty-fourth section of said chapter is hereby amended by striking out therefrom the word "four."

SEC. 15. The eighty-fifth section of said chapter is hereby amended so as to read as follows:

Superintendent of buildings.

§ 85. There shall be a department called the "department of buildings," which shall be under the control of an officer who shall be known as the "superintendent of buildings," and shall be the same person nominated as "commissioner of buildings" by the mayor of the city of

New York, on the fifteenth day of May, one thousand eight hundred and seventy-three, and confirmed by the board of aldermen of said city, on the sixteenth day of May, one thousand eight hundred and seventy-three; which said superintendent shall hold office for the full term for which said commissioner was appointed, unless sooner removed, as provided by law, for the removal of heads of departments.

The eighty-sixth section of said chapter is hereby amended so as to read as follows:

Department of buildings, powers and duties.

§ 86. Each and all the powers and duties of said department, and all its officers and employees and subordinates, and their qualifications, shall continue and be exercised as non-authorized by special laws in relation to buildings in the city of New York, and it shall not be lawful for any officer or employee in said department to be engaged in conducting or carrying on business as an architect, carpenter, mason or builder while holding office in said department. The one hundred and sixteenth section of said chapter is hereby amended by striking out therefrom the words "to the commissioner" and "surveyor" of buildings four thousand dollars "each," and inserting in lieu thereof "to the superintendent of buildings four thousand dollars." Fees.

SEC. 16. Section ninety-six of said chapter is hereby amended by inserting after the word "government," in the first line thereof, the following words, viz., "except the city marshals." Said section is hereby further amended by adding at the end thereof the following: "But nothing herein contained shall be construed so as to repeal, modify or otherwise affect the provisions of the fourteenth section of chapter seven hundred and forty-two of the laws of eighteen hundred and seventy-one."

Sale or lease of market property.

SEC. 17. Section one hundred and two is hereby amended by inserting in the third section thereof, after the words, but if said property be "market property," the following words, viz., "excepting the market between Sixteenth and Seventeenth streets, east of Avenue C, the market in Governeur slip, and the market in Old slip."

SEC. 18. Section one hundred and three of said chapter is hereby repealed.

SEC. 19. Section one hundred and eleven of the said chapter is hereby amended by adding at the end thereof the following:

Printing and stationery.

"Nothing herein contained shall apply to any printing or supplies of stationery for any department where, by the concurrent vote of the mayor, commissioner of public works, and corporation counsel, it shall be decided to have such printing done or such stationery furnished without contract; but in such cases such printing and stationery shall be procured in such manner and on such terms and conditions as the said officers shall deem to be for the best interests of the city."

SEC. 20. Section one hundred and twelve of said chapter is hereby amended by inserting in the first sentence of the same, after the words "and branch thereof," the following words, viz., "and the board of education;" and also by inserting in the fourth sentence, after the words "the heads of departments," the following words, viz., "and the board of education." The said section is hereby further amended by adding at the end thereof the following:

Unexpended balances of appropriation.

"Any balances of appropriations remaining unexpended, after allowing sufficient to satisfy all claims payable therefrom, may, at any time, after the expiration of the year for which they were made, be transferred by the comptroller, with the approval of said board of estimate and apportionment, to the general fund of the city, and applied to the reduction of taxation."

SEC. 21. Section one hundred and fourteen of said chapter shall not be construed to apply to civil or consulting engineers who may be appointed to superintend any specific work on the part of the city of New York.

SEC. 22. Section one hundred and fifteen of said chapter is hereby amended so as to read as follows:

Repaving streets, etc., at expense of owners, to be done only on petition.

§ 115. No street, avenue, or public place in the city of New York, which has been once paved, and the expense thereof paid for by the owners of the adjoining property, by assessment, shall hereafter be paved at their expense, nor shall any assessment therefor be imposed, unless the same shall be petitioned for by a majority of the owners of the property (who shall also be the owners of a majority of the front feet) on the line of the proposed improvement; and any ordinance or resolution heretofore passed for any repavement, which has not been petitioned for by a majority of the owners of the adjoining property to be affected, and for which no contract has been entered into or award of contract made, is hereby declared to be inoperative and void. Except for repairs, no patented pavement shall be laid, and no patented article shall be advertised for, contracted for, or purchased, except under such circumstances that there can be a fair and reasonable opportunity for competition, the conditions to secure which shall be prescribed by the board of estimate and apportionment.

SEC. 23. That portion of section one hundred and sixteen of said chapter referring to the salary of members of the board of aldermen and members of the board of assistant aldermen, and that portion of said section referring to the salary of the president of board of aldermen, are hereby amended so as to read as follows:

To the members of the board of aldermen, other than the president, four thousand dollars each; and to the members of the board of assistant aldermen, four thousand dollars each, during their present term of office. Salaries.

To the president of the board of aldermen, five thousand dollars.

That portion of said section referring to the salary of the commissioner of accounts is hereby amended so as to read as follows: Salaries of commissioners of accounts.

To the commissioners of accounts appointed by the mayor, three thousand dollars each.

The last subdivision of said section one hundred and sixteen is hereby amended so as to read as follows:

No subordinate in any department shall receive a greater salary than the highest salary paid to the head of the department, except the superintendent of the police, whose salary shall not exceed ten thousand dollars per annum.

Salary of justices.

The salary of the justices of the district courts is hereby fixed at eight thousand dollars each per annum.

Sec. 24. Section one hundred and twenty of said chapter is hereby amended by striking out therefrom the words "in section one hundred and twenty-two," and inserting in place thereof the words "in section one hundred and seventeen."

Sec. 25. This act shall take effect immediately.

(E.)

Chapter 129.

An Act to amend an act entitled "An act to reorganize the local government of the city of New York," passed April thirtieth, eighteen hundred and seventy-three.

Passed April 21, 1875; three-fifths being present.

The People of the State of New York, represented in Senate and Assembly, do enact as follows:

Section 1. Section thirty-five of chapter three hundred and thirty-five of the laws of eighteen hundred and seventy-three, entitled "An act to reorganize the local government of the city of New York," passed April thirtieth, eighteen hundred and seventy-three, is hereby amended so as to read as follows:

City chamberlain, duties of.

§ 35. The said chamberlain and mayor and the comptroller of the city of New York, shall, by a majority vote, by written notice, to the comptroller, designate the banks or trust companies in which all moneys of the mayor, aldermen, and commonalty of the said city and county of New York shall be deposited, and may, by like notice, in writing, from time to time, change the banks or trust companies thus designated; but no such bank or trust company shall be designated

unless its officers shall agree to pay into the city treasury interest on the daily balances at a rate to be fixed by the mayor and chamberlain, and the said comptroller of the city of New York, by a majority vote, which rate shall not be less than two and one-half per cent. The said chamberlain shall keep books showing the receipts of moneys from all sources, and designating the sources of the same, and also showing the amounts paid from time to time on account of the several appropriations; and no warrant shall be paid on account of any appropriation after the amount authorized to be raised for that specific purpose shall have been expended. The said chamberlain shall once in each week report in writing to the mayor and to the comptroller all moneys received by him, the amounts of all warrants paid by him since his last report, and the amount remaining to the credit of the city and county of New York respectively. The said chamberlain shall receive the sum of thirty thousand dollars annually, and no more, for all his services as Salary.
chamberlain of said city and as county treasurer of the county of New York in lieu of salary and of all interest, fees, commissions and emoluments; and all such interest, fees, commissions and emoluments shall be accounted for and paid over by him to the city treasury. He may appoint and remove at pleasure, a deputy chamberlain and such clerks May appoint clerks.
and assistants as may be necessary, whose salaries, together with all the expenses of his office, shall be paid wholly by him, and shall in no case be a public charge. The commissions provided by law, and received by him for receiving and paying over the state taxes, and all interest accrued on deposits shall be paid by him to the commissioners of the sinking fund.

SEC. 2. This act shall take effect immediately.

(F.)

Chapter 300.

An Act to amend chapter three hundred and thirty-five of the laws of eighteen hundred and seventy-three, entitled "An act to reorganize the local government of the city of New York," passed April thirtieth, eighteen hundred and seventy-three, and the acts amendatory thereof.

Passed April 30, 1874; three-fifths being present.

The People of the State of New York, represented in Senate and Assembly, do enact as follows:

Section 1. Section thirty-nine of chapter three hundred and thirty-five of the laws of eighteen hundred and seventy-three, entitled "An act to reorganize the local government of the city of New York," passed April thirtieth, eighteen hundred and seventy-three, is hereby amended so as to read as follows:

Appointment of police commissioners.

§ 39. The police department shall have for its head a board to consist of four persons, to be known as police commissioners of the city of New York, who shall, except those first appointed, hold their offices for six years, unless sooner removed as herein provided. The office of the police commissioner of the city of New York, whose term of office expires on the first day of May, eighteen hundred and seventy-four, is hereby abolished on and after said date; the police department, on and after the first day of May, eighteen hundred and seventy-four, shall be under the charge and control of four commissioners, who shall perform all the duties and exercise all the powers now by law conferred or imposed upon the police deparment of the city of New York.

Sec. 2. Section eighty-four of chapter three hundred and thirty-five of the laws of eighteen hundred and seventy-three, entitled "An act to reorganize the local government of the city of New York," passed April thirtieth, eighteen hundred and seventy-three, is hereby amended so as to read as follows:

Park commissioners.

§ 84. This department shall be under the charge of a board, to consist of four members, who, except those first appointed, shall hold their offices for five years, unless sooner removed as herein provided. The office of the commissioner of parks, whose term of office expires on the first day of May, eighteen hundred and seventy-four, is hereby abolished on and after said date. The department of public parks on and after the first day of May, eighteen hundred and seventy-four, shall be under the charge and control of four commissioners, who shall perform all the duties and exercise all ths powers now by law conferred or imposed upon the department of public parks of the city of New York.

Office of commissioner of parks abolished.

Vacancies, how filled.

SEC. 3. The mayor of said city shall hereafter appoint, without confirmation of the board of aldermen, a person or persons to fill any vacancy or vacancies which now exists or may hereafter occur from death, resignation or cause other than the expiration of the full term in any office to which, of the provisions of the twenty-fifth section of chapter three hundred and thirty-five of the laws of eighteen hundred and seventy-three, he is empowered to appoint by and with the consent of the board of aldermen.

SEC. 4 This act shall take effect immediately

(G.)

Chapter 476.

AN ACT to provide for a uniform system for the repavement of streets, avenues, and public places in the city of New York.

Passed May 28, 1875; three-fifths being present.

The People of the State of New York, represented in Senate and Assembly, do enact as follows:

Powers of board of aldermen to direct repavement of streets and avenues.

SECTION 1. Whenever the commissioner of public works of the city of New York shall certify and report to the board of aldermen of said city that the safety, health, or convenience of the public requires the repavement of any streets, avenues, or public places in said city, said board of aldermen shall have the power to direct by ordinance or resolution the repavement of said streets, avenues, or public places, in the manner specified and of the materials approved of and recommended by said commissioner of public works, which work shall be done by and under the direction of the department of public works, according to law. In case any of the streets, avenues, or public places in said city shall have been once paved, and the expense thereof assessed upon the owners of adjoining and benefited property, the cost of the repaving thereof shall be borne by a general assessment upon all taxable property in said city. The cost of repaving the streets, avenues, or public places, in accordance with the provisions of this act, shall be included in the estimate of the department of public works, shall be appropriated by the board of estimate and apportionment, certified by the comptroller according to law, and inserted and included in the annual tax levies, and raised and collected by tax upon the estates subject to taxation in the city and county of New York, provided that the amount so appropriated and raised shall not exceed the sum of five hundred thousand dollars in any one single year.

Materials.

Work done under direction of department of public works.

The cost of repaving raised and collected by tax.

SEC. 2. All acts and parts of acts which are inconsistent with the provisions of this act are hereby repealed so far as they relate to this act.

SEC. 3. This act shall take effect immediately.

(H.)

Chapter 726.

AN ACT to provide for the more effectual extinguishment of fires in the city of New York.

Passed June 12, 1873; three-fifths being present.

The People of the State of New York, represented in Senate and Assembly, do enact as follows:

SECTION 1. The fire commissioners of the city of New York are hereby empowered and directed to organize, in the fire department of the city of New York, a corps to be known as the corps of sappers and miners. Said corps shall be composed of not exceeding three members, either officers or private firemen, of each company in said fire department, and said members shall be appointed by said fire commissioners, upon the nomination of the chief engineer of said fire department. Fire department to organize corps of sappers and miners.

SEC. 2. The said fire commissioners shall appoint a suitable officer, who shall be skilled in the use of explosives, whose duty it shall be to instruct and drill said corps in the use of explosives, and to give said corps such other instruction as may be required to qualify them to effectually discharge the duties imposed upon them by this act. Such officer shall receive an annual salary of two thousand dollars, and such salary shall be raised and paid in the same manner as the salaries of the other officers appointed by the said fire commissioners. Drill officer to be appointed. Salary.

SEC. 3. Whenever, under and by virtue of the acts relating to the extinguishment of fires in the said city of New York, the destruction or pulling down of any building or buildings shall be deemed necessary, and shall be ordered by the engineer in command at any fire in said city, it shall be the duty of said corps, or any member or members thereof, by the direction of the said engineer in command at such fire, to level and destroy such building or buildings by the use of explosives, for the purpose of arresting the spread of such fire, and it shall be lawful for them to enter and take possession of the same for such purposes.

Duties of sappers and miners.

Depots for storage of explosives.

SEC. 4. The said fire commissioners shall establish in the city of New York one or more depots for the storage and safe keeping of such explosives as may be required for the use of said corps, and may limit the quantity of any such explosives to be kept at any one of such depots.

SEC. 5. All acts or portions of acts inconsistent with the provisions of this act are hereby repealed.

SEC. 6. This act shall take effect immediately.

(I.)

Chapter 839.

AN ACT to authorize the board of health of the health department of the city of New York to make a contract to remove the contents of sinks and privies in said city.

Passed June 26, 1873; three-fifths being present.

The People of the State of New York, represented in Senate and Assembly, do enact as follows:

Board of health authorized to contract for removing contents of sinks and privies.

SECTION 1. The board of health of the health department of the city of New York is hereby authorized to contract with any responsible person or persons, up to the first of May, eighteen hundred and seventy-five (or the sooner determination of a contract made by and between the mayor, aldermen, and commonalty of said city of the one part, and Daniel Gallagher of the other part, bearing date May first, eighteen hundred and sixty-five, by which the former agreed, among other things, to deliver to the latter all the contents of sinks and privies, as therein specified, until the first of May, eighteen hundred and seventy-five), to furnish during the day, as well as the night, the necessary boats for receiving and removing, and to remove and deliver all the contents of sinks and privies, as Thomas Andrews, by a contract, between him and the mayor, aldermen, and commonalty of said city, bearing date May first, eighteen hundred and sixty-five, agreed to furnish for receiving and removing, and to remove and deliver such contents, and in relation thereto, at a price not exceeding thirty-three thousand dollars per annum, to be paid in equal monthly installments, and to require and receive satisfactory security in such form and amount as such board may approve for the faithful performance, by the person or persons to whom such contract may be awarded, of all and every of the provisions of such contract on his or their part. For any breach of said contract by such contracting party or parties, an action may be prosecuted in the name of the mayor, alderman,* and commonalty of the city of New York, in any court having jurisdiction thereof, against said party or parties, his or their sureties, or both, to recover the damages sustained by such breach or breaches, as the same may from time to time occur; but nothing in this section contained shall be construed to legalize the contract or contracts for the purposes herein stated.

Penalty for breach of contract.

SEC. 2. This act shall take effect immediately.

* So in original.

(J.)

Chapter 759.

An Act to provide for the completion of county buildings in the city and county of New York.

Passed June 13, 1873; three-fifths being present.

The People of the State of New York, represented in Senate and Assembly, do enact as follows:

Commissioners of buildings.

Section 1. The terms of office of each and every commissioner heretofore appointed for the erection of buildings for county purposes in the city and county of New York shall be and are hereby declared to be terminated. And the persons nominated by the mayor of the city of New York, and by and with the consent of the board of aldermen appointed as such commissioners, pursuant to chapter three hundred and thirty-five of the laws of eighteen hundred and seventy-three, shall be commissioners for the purposes for which they are appointed, and shall have and perform all the powers and duties given to such commissioners by the existing provisions of law. The compensation of such commissioners shall be fixed by the board of estimate and apportionment, but shall in no case exceed the sum of two thousand dollars each per annum.

How appointed.

Powers and duties.

Compensation.

Sec. 2. This act shall take effect immediately.

(K.)

Chapter 631.

AN ACT to amend chapter seven hundred and fifty-seven of the laws of eighteen hundred and seventy-three, entitled "An act to amend chapter three hundred and thirty-five of the laws of eighteen hundred and seventy-three, entitled 'An act to reorganize the local government of the city of New York,'" passed April thirteenth, eighteen hundred and seventy-three.

Passed June 21, 1875; three-fifths being present.

The People of the State of New York, represented in Senate and Assembly, do enact as follows:

SECTION 1. Section nineteen of chapter seven hundred and fifty-seven of the laws of eighteen hundred and seventy-three, entitled "An act to amend chapter three hundred and thirty-five of the laws of eighteen hundred and seventy-three, entitled 'An act to reorganize the local government of the city of New York,'" passed April thirteenth, eighteen hundred and seventy-three, is hereby amended so as to read as follows:

Printing, etc., otherwise than by contract.

§ 19. Section one hundred and eleven of the said chapter is hereby amended by adding at the end thereof the following: "Nothing herein contained shall apply to any printing or supplies of stationery for the mayor, aldermen, and commonalty of the city of New York, where, by the concurrent vote of the mayor, counsel to the corporation, and the commissioner of public works, it shall be decided to have such printing done or such stationery furnished without contract let after advertisements for bids or proposals; but in such cases such printing shall be done and such stationery procured in the manner, and on such terms and conditions as the said officers shall deem to be for the best interests of the city."

SEC. 2. This act shall take effect immediately.

(L.)

Chapter 758.

An Act in relation to the city of New York.

Passed June 13, 1873; three-fifths being present.

The People of the State of New York, represented in Senate and Assembly, do enact as follows:

Powers of board of estimate and apportionment.

Section 1. The board of estimate and apportionment constituted by section one hundred and twelve of chapter three hundred and thirty-five of the laws of eighteen hundred and seventy-three, is hereby authorized at any time before the first day of July next, by the concurrent vote of all the members of said board, to reconsider, revise and redetermine any estimate made under the provisions of section eight of chapter five hundred and seventy-four of the laws of eighteen hundred and seventy-one, and the estimates so reconsidered, revised and redetermined and approved by the concurrent vote of all the members of said board, shall thereby become appropriated as the amount of money required to defray all the various expenses necessary for conducting the various boards, commissions and departments, whether executive, judicial, legislative or administrative, of the city government, and also for paying the interest on the city debt, and the principal of such debt falling due, and for providing for charitable or other objects, and said amount shall be established and be the amount to be raised for such purposes by tax within the city and county of New York for the year eighteen hundred and seventy-three, and the amount thus established shall be certified to the board of supervisors by the comptroller, and the said board of supervisors are hereby empowered and directed to cause the amount so certified to be raised and collected in the year eighteen hundred and seventy-three by tax upon estates,

Supervisors to raise amount appropriated by taxation.

real and personal, within the city and county of New York subject to taxation.

SEC. 2. Nothing contained in any act heretofore passed shall prevent the payment of arrears of rent for armories and drill-rooms in cases in which the board of supervisors, since the first day of January, eighteen hundred and seventy-two, shall have authorized the leases of such armories and drill-rooms to be canceled and the public use thereof to cease, on condition of the payment of such arrears of rents, or in cases in which the premises shall have been continuously occupied as armories or drill-rooms until the present time, or until the expiration of the terms for which the same were leased. Arrears of rent for armories and drill-rooms.

SEC. 3. Nothing contained in section one hundred and eleven of chapter three hundred and thirty-five of the laws of eighteen hundred and seventy-three, shall prevent the publication of any advertisement required by law; provided, however, that no such publication shall be made unless the same is authorized by a concurrent vote of the mayor, corporation counsel and commissioner of public works. Advertising

SEC. 4. This act shall take effect immediately.

(M.)

Chapter 308.

AN ACT in relation to the estimates and apportionments for the support of the government of the city of New York.

Passed May 1, 1874; three-fifths being present.

The People of the State of New York, represented in Senate and Assembly, do enact as follows:

SECTION 1. The board of estimate and apportionment constituted by section one hundred and twelve of chapter three hundred and thirty-five of the laws of eighteen hundred and seventy-three, is hereby authorized, at any time before the first day of July, eighteen hundred and seventy-four, by the concurrent vote of all the members of said board, to reconsider, revise, and redetermine the estimate for the year eighteen hundred and seventy-four, heretofore made under the provisions of said act, and of section twenty of chapter seven hundred and fifty-seven of the laws of eighteen hundred and seventy-three, and the amount of the estimate so reconsidered, revised, and redetermined and approved by the concurrent vote of all the members of said board, shall thereby become appropriated as the amount of money required to defray the expenses of conducting the public business of the city of New York and of the various departments, boards, and commissions thereof, whether administrative, executive, or judicial, and for paying the interest on the city debt and the principal of such debt falling due in and for the year eighteen hundred and seventy-four, and for all liabilities of the city of New York, by reason of the annexation thereto of territory lately a part of Westchester county, and for the expenses of conducting the public business of said annexed territory for and during said year, and the liabilities incurred by the board of education of said territory during the year eighteen hundred and seventy-three, which are hereby made an obligation of the city of New York; and the aggregate amount of said estimate, after deducting the estimated amount of the revenues of the general fund of the city of New York, not otherwise specifically appropriated by law, including surplus revenues of the sinking fund for the payment of interest on the city debt, shall be established and be the amount to be raised for all such purposes, by tax, within the city and county of New York for the year eighteen hundred and seventy-four, and the amount thus established shall be certified to the board of supervisors by the comptroller; and the said board of supervisors are hereby empowered and directed to cause the amount so certified to be raised and collected in the year eighteen hundred and seventy-four, by tax upon the estates by law subject to taxation within the city and county of New York. But the aggregate amount of the estimates for the year eighteen hundred and seventy-four, to be made by the said board of estimate and apportionment, shall not exceed the amount of the estimate heretofore

Estimate for 1874 to be revised and corrected.

Taxes, how appropriated.

Apportionments, when certified, to be raised by tax.

made by the said board, as aforesaid. In the estimate, so to be made, no sum shall be included, except the same be appropriated for a specified department or purpose, and no sum shall be appropriated for special contingencies.

Special contingencies.

SEC. 2. The said board of estimate and apportionment shall have the power at any time to transfer any appropriation for any year which may be found, by the head of the department for which such appropriation shall have been made, to be in excess of the amount required or deemed to be necessary for the purposes or objects thereof, to such other purposes or objects for which the appropriations are insufficient, or such as may require the same ; and if it is found at the time when the estimate is made of the expenses of conducting the public business of the city of New York for the next succeeding fiscal year, that there will be a surplus or balance remaining unexpended of any appropriation then existing at the end of the current fiscal year, such surplus may be applied to like purposes in the next succeeding year.

Unexpended appropriations may be transferred.

SEC. 3. The amount of money required by provision of section eight of chapter seven hundred and two of the laws of eighteen hundred and seventy-two, to be included in the amount to be raised by tax in the year eighteen hundred and seventy-three, by section four of chapter ninety-five, laws of eighteen hundred and seventy-three, to be included in the amount to be raised by tax in the year eighteen hundred and seventy-four, shall, instead of being raised in eighteen hundred and seventy-four, be raised and included in the amount to be levied by tax in the year eighteen hundred and seventy-five ; and in anticipation of the levy and collection thereof, the comptroller is authorized and required to issue revenue bonds for such amounts as may from time to time be required to be paid pursuant to the provisions of section seven of said chapter seven hundred and two of the laws of eighteen hundred and seventy-two, such revenue bonds to be paid from the amounts so to be raised by tax in the year eighteen hundred and seventy-five. This act shall not be construed to authorize said board to reduce or transfer any appropriation heretofore or hereafter made for the purposes of carrying out the provisions of the acts mentioned in this section; and

Comptroller to issue revenue bonds in lieu of taxes for 1874.

except as herein modified, all the provisions of chapter seven hundred and two of the laws of eighteen hundred and seventy-two are confirmed and continued in full force and effect.

Tax levy for 1874 limited.

SEC. 4. No moneys shall be levied and raised in the year eighteen hundred and seventy-four by tax within the county of New York for the purposes authorized by section seventeen of chapter five hundred and thirty-five of the laws of eighteen hundred and seventy-three, excepting such expenses as may have been actually incurred by the commission in said act named.

SEC. 5. This act shall take effect immediately.

(N.)

Chapter 303.

AN ACT in relation to the estimates and apportionment for the support of the government of the county of New York.

Passed April 30, 1874; three-fifths being present.

The People of the State of New York, represented in Senate and Assembly, do enact as follows:

Estimate and appropriations, how levied and collected.

SECTION 1. The board of estimate and apportionment constituted by section one of chapter seven hundred and seventy-nine of the laws of eighteen hundred and seventy-three, is hereby authorized by a concurrent vote of all the members thereof, at any time before the first day of July, eighteen hundred and seventy-four, to reconsider, revise, and redetermine the estimate heretofore made under the provisions of said act for the year eighteen hundred and seventy-four, and the estimates so reconsidered, revised, and redetermined and approved by the concurrent vote of all said members, shall thereby be appropriated as the amount of money required to defray all the various expenses necessary for conducting the county government, and for supporting inmates of asylums, reformatories, and charitable institutions chargeable by existing provisions of law upon the county of New York, and for defraying all legal charges against the county of New York under special laws, and also for paying the interest on the county debt and the principal of such debt falling due in the year eighteen hundred and seventy-four, and the proportion of the state tax for the year eighteen hundred and seventy-four payable by said county, and thereupon to fix and determine the amount of such estimates and various expenses and charges after deducting the estimated amount of county revenue not otherwise appropriated by law, which amount, when so fixed and determined, shall be certified to the board of supervisors of the county of New York by the Comptroller; and said board of supervisors are hereby empowered and directed to cause the amount so certified, to be levied and collected in the year eighteen hundred and seventy-four, by tax upon the estates within the county of New York subject to taxation. But the aggregate amount of the estimate for the year eighteen hundred and seventy-four, to be made by the said board of estimate and apportionment, shall not exceed the amount of the estimate heretofore made by the said board as aforesaid. In the estimate so to be made no sum shall be included, except the same be appropriated for a specified department or purpose, and no sum shall be appropriated for special contingencies.

Estimates for 1874 limited.

SEC. 2. The said board of estimate and apportionment shall have the power at any time to transfer any appropriatian for any year which may be found by the head of the department for which such appropriation shall have been made to be in excess of the amount required or deemed to be necessary for the purposes or objects thereof, to such other purposes or objects for which the appropriations are insufficient, or such as may require the same; and if it is found at the time when the estimate is made of the expenses of conducting the public business of the county of New York for the next succeeding fiscal year, that there will be a surplus or balance remaining unexpended of any appropriation then existing at the end of the current fiscal year, such surplus may be applied to like purposes in the next succeeding year.

Appropriations may be transferred.

Change of time for paying installment on bonds.

SEC. 3. The payment of the bonds authorized by section three of chapter ninety-five of the laws of eighteen hundred and seventy-three, instead of commencing in the year eighteen hundred and seventy-four, as therein provided, shall have the first installment thereof paid in the year eighteen hundred and seventy-six, and the other installments annually thereafter.

SEC. 4. This act shall take effect immediately.

(O.)

Chapter 326.

AN ACT to limit in certain respects the effect of certain repealing clauses in a bill which has passed the Senate and Assembly, at the present session, entitled "An act to reorganize the local government of the city of New York," so that such bill shall, as a law, conform to the intent of the legislature.

Passed April 29, 1873; three-fifths being present.

The People of the State of New York, represented in Senate and Assembly, do enact as follows:

Indictments and prosecutions.

SECTION 1. Nothing contained in the bill or act entitled "An act to reorganize the local government of the city of New York," passed at this session of the legislature, shall affect any right heretofore accrued or liability heretofore incurred, or prevent the indictment, or prosecution under indictments found or to be found, of any person or persons, for any offense or offenses heretofore committed, and all such rights, liabilities and offenses shall remain subject to redress, enforcement and punishment in like manner as if the acts so repealed as aforesaid had remained in full force.

SEC. 2. This act shall take effect immediately.

GENERAL INDEX.

A

B

C

D

F

G

H

I

J

L

M

N

O

P

POWERS AND DUTIES OF—

PRESIDENT OF—

Q

R

S

www.ingramcontent.com/pod-product-compliance
Lightning Source LLC
LaVergne TN
LVHW021402110826
845150LV00007B/1753

* 9 7 8 1 4 2 5 5 1 2 6 9 9 *